ESSENT

FLORIDA

Original text by Emma Stanford
Updated by Gary McKechnie

© Automobile Association Developments Limited 2008
First published 2008

ISBN 978-0-7495-5360-9

Published by AA Publishing, a trading name of Automobile Association Developments
Limited, whose registered office is Fanum House, Basing View, Basingstoke,
Hampshire RG21 4EA.
Registered number 1878835.

Automobile Association Developments Limited retains the copyright in the original
edition © 1998 and in all subsequent editions, reprints and amendments

A CIP catalogue record for this book is available from the British Library

Colour separation: MRM Graphics Ltd
Printed and bound in Italy by Printer Trento S.r.l.

A03164
Maps in this title produced from mapping © MAIRDUMONT / Falk Verlag 2007

About this book

Symbols are used to denote the following categories:

➕ map reference to maps on cover

✉ address or location

☎ telephone number

🕐 opening times

💷 admission charge

🍴 restaurant or café on premises or nearby

Ⓜ nearest underground train station

🚍 nearest bus/tram route

🚆 nearest overground train station

⛴ nearest ferry stop

✈ nearest airport

❓ other practical information

ℹ tourist information office

➤ indicates the page where you will find a fuller description

This book is divided into six sections.

The essence of Florida pages 6–19
Introduction; Features; Food and drink; and Short break

Planning pages 20–33
Before you go; Getting there; Getting around; Being there

Best places to see pages 34–55
The unmissable highlights of any visit to Florida

Best things to do pages 56–71
Great places to have lunch; Top beaches; Alternative attractions and more

Exploring pages 72–186
The best places to visit in Florida, organized by area

🔶 to 🔶🔶🔶🔶🔶 denotes AAA rating

Maps
All map references are to the maps on the covers. For example, Miami Beach has the reference ➕ 17R – indicating the grid square in which it is to be found

Admission prices
Inexpensive (under $10);
Moderate ($10–$20);
Expensive ($20–$35);
Very expensive (over $35)

Hotel prices
Price are per room per night: **$** budget (under $100); **$$** moderate ($100–180); **$$$** expensive to luxury (over $180)

Restaurant prices
Price for a three-course meal per person without drinks: **$** budget (under $20); **$$** moderate ($20–$35); **$$$** expensive (over $35)

Contents

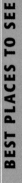

The essence of...

Florida is quite a phenomenon. It took less than a century for the former pestilential swamp state to reinvent itself as one of the most important vacation destinations of modern times, an alluring combination of sun, sea, sand, palm trees and theme parks.

There is, however, another Florida, one blessed with weird and wonderful wildlife and a surprising history preserved in ancient shell mounds, Spanish forts and fancy Victorian historic districts. Step briefly off the beaten track, usually no more than 10 minutes off the highway, and you will find the quirky and intriguing essence of the "Real Florida".

features

It is a popular misconception that Florida's charms are limited to its famous theme parks and its beautiful beaches. While the Sunshine State can certainly lay claim to some of the best of both in the world, there is a great deal more to engage first-time, third-time or even serial visitors.

Florida makes an ideal two-center vacation destination. A week of theme parking in Orlando is just about all the human body can survive – and afford. This is the one time Florida sightseeing gets seriously expensive. Beyond the theme parks there is a terrific choice of beachfront resorts and golf courses, and the contrasting attractions of glitzy Miami, with its Latin American pizazz, and the laid-back Florida Keys. Northern Florida is a well-kept secret, reminiscent of the Old South. Here, you will find a perceptible change of pace, historical sites and awesome beaches.

GEOGRAPHY

● A low-lying, limestone peninsula bordered by Georgia and Alabama to the north, Florida is the 22nd largest state in the US at 58,625 sq miles.

● From the Georgia border, it is just over 420 miles (672km) due south to Key West, which is the most southerly point of the continental US, and a mere 90 miles (146km) to Cuba.

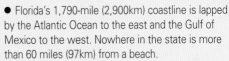

- Florida's 1,790-mile (2,900km) coastline is lapped by the Atlantic Ocean to the east and the Gulf of Mexico to the west. Nowhere in the state is more than 60 miles (97km) from a beach.
- Average temperatures during summer vary little and range from 81°F (27°C) to 82°F (28°C) across the state. Average winter temperatures are between 53°F (11.5°C) and 68°F (20°C).
- The state capital is Tallahassee.

ECONOMY

- Tourism is Florida's number one industry. In 2005, an estimated 83.6 million visitors (4.4 million from outside the US) arrived in Florida.
- Agriculture is the second largest earner, chiefly sugar cane, timber, and citrus fruits. Florida supplies over 70 percent of the US citrus harvest.

CONCHS AND CRACKERS

It sounds like a Floridian snack food, but Conchs and Crackers are in fact original Florida residents. As well as being an edible mollusc, a Conch (pronounced "conk") is a Florida Keys resident, born and bred. A Cracker is a descendant of the pioneer farmers, named for the cracking of their cowmen's whips, or for the cracked corn used to make grits.

PEOPLE

Florida's population of around 16.7 million is concentrated in the south and coastal cities. Cracker farmers mostly live in the north. Down south there is a large, powerful Cuban community in Miami joined by more recent refugees from Haiti, Nicaragua, and other Latin American countries. Florida's Native American population is also based down south. The Seminole and smaller Miccosukee tribes operate semiautonomous reservations in and around the Everglades.

food & drink

The first rule of eating out in Florida is make sure you are hungry. From the awesome heights of an all-American breakfast to the mile-high Cuban sandwich at lunch and a fresh seafood dinner at the end of a busy day's sightseeing, Florida portion control errs well beyond the realms of simple generosity.

FLORIDA SPECIALTIES

In recent years, some of Florida's finest chefs have been perfecting "Floribbean" cuisine, a delicious fusion of fresh local produce and more exotic Caribbean flavors with a bit of New American and Asian flair thrown in. Otherwise, there are few typically Floridian dishes on the menu, but nobody should miss out on a chance to sample *real* Key lime pie, which should be yellow not green.

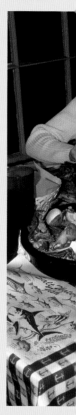

Down in the Keys, conch fritters or chowder (a rather chewy seafood stew) are local dishes. Farmed alligator meat is usually served well disguised as deep-fried nuggets, but if it appears on the menu in a good restaurant it is well worth trying, and is not dissimilar to chicken.

In northern Florida there are plenty of opportunities to sample Southern-style cooking. Grits (a sloppy cornmeal porridge best served with salt, pepper and butter) is something of an acquired taste, but barbecued meats are delicious, and look out for "blackened" dishes, which are coated with tangy Cajun-style spices.

SEAFOOD

Seafood restaurants abound in Florida. Snapper, grouper, yellowtail and pompano are among the top locally caught fish, and dolphin, also known as mahi-mahi, which is a fish not a performing mammal. In southern Florida, stone crabs are harvested from October to April, and in the Panhandle, shrimps, blue crabs and oysters are local treats.

CUBAN COOKING

The Latin American influence is strongest in the southern part of the state, particularly Miami. This is the place to sample a Cuban sandwich served in a long roll packed with cheese, ham, and pork, and a strong, sweet *café cubano*, a

thimble-sized cup of coffee that more than lives up to its nickname: zoom juice. Favorite restaurant dishes include chicken with rice *(arroz con pollo)* and fried beef *(vaca frita)* served with black beans, rice and fried plantain.

BUDGET BITES

It is easy to eat out cheaply and well in Florida. Resort areas generally offer a wide choice of family restaurants and familiar fast food chains. Look out for special deals such as Early Bird menus served before the main evening rush, and all-you-can-eat fixed-price buffets. Larger shopping malls generally offer a food court with a selection of different cafés and takeout operations serving anything from pizza and deli sandwiches to Chinese and Tex-Mex dishes. Good ready-made meals and salads are sold in supermarkets, and buying up cold drinks at supermarket prices can save a small fortune.

DRINKING

Soft drinks are widely available and vacationers should be sure to drink plenty in

order to avoid dehydration in the hot Florida sunshine.

The legal age to drink alcohol is 21 and identification may be required as proof. Wine and beer are available in supermarkets, but spirits can only be bought in a liquor store.

short break

If you only have a short time to visit Florida, or would like to get a really complete picture of the region, here are the essentials:

● **Get a tan** – but however short your stay, treat the Florida sun with respect. Take it very gently and use a high factor sunscreen. If you do burn take comfort by using soothing aloe vera gel, a local product.

● **Ride a roller coaster** – you have not done Florida until you have sampled a roller-coaster ride. Some of the best are found at Tampa's Busch Gardens (➤ 135).

● **Visit a state park** – not only a chance to get to grips with the great outdoors, but many of Florida's state parks also protect historical sites.

● **Bring a snorkel** – as well as a live coral reef off the Florida Keys, there are numerous dive sites around the state.

● **Watch a sunset** – sunset celebrations are big news on the Gulf Coast. Mallory Square in Key West (➤ 40–41) hosts the most famous nightly sunset party.

● **Take a boat trip** – nature trips, canoe adventures, fishing expeditions and sunset sails; it is easy to take to the water in Florida.

● **Collect shells** – beaches on the Gulf of Mexico are the best for shell collecting, particularly the islands of Sanibel and Captiva (➤ 50–51).

● **Meet a manatee** – either in the wild or at rescue and rehabilitation units within aquariums, such as SeaWorld (➤ 131) and the Miami Seaquarium (➤ 83).

● **Travel into space** – only the very wealthy can sign up for a Shuttle trip, but the next best thing is to watch a launch from the Kennedy Space Center (► 38–39).

● **Take mosquito repellent** – absolutely essential when visiting parks and reserves. Mosquitoes love humid, jungly swamps and woodland areas.

Planning

Before you go

WHEN TO GO

JAN	FEB	MAR	APR	MAY	JUN	JUL	AUG	SEP	OCT	NOV	DEC
22°C	23°C	25°C	27°C	27°C	30°C	32°C	32°C	30°C	28°C	25°C	22°C
72°F	73°F	77°F	81°F	81°F	86°F	90°F	90°F	86°F	82°F	77°F	72°F

🔵 High season ⚪ Low season

Temperatures above are the average daily maximum for each month. At night temperatures fall to 70–75°F (21–24°C). Florida has a subtropical climate: it is warm and extremely hot and humid in summer. Cooling sea breezes help to dissipate the summer heat of Miami and Tampa (77–86°F/25–30°C). Winter temperatures in Central Florida are a little cooler than in the southern part of the state.

In Orlando the summer heat is more stifling and the humidity can become inbearable. During summer (June to September), most mornings are sunny, but expect afternoon thunderstorms which cool temperatures off a little. Few days in February and March are cloudy all day. Best times to visit Orlando are October and early May.

WHAT YOU NEED

		UK	Germany	USA	Netherlands	Spain
● Required	Contact your travel agent or the US embassy for the current regulations regarding passports and the Visa Waiver Form/Visa. Your passport should be valid for at least six months beyond date of entry.					
○ Suggested						
▲ Not required						
Passport/National Identity Card (Valid for 6 months after entry)		●	●	▲	●	●
Visa Waiver Form		●	●	▲	●	●
Onward or Return Ticket		●	●	▲	●	●
Health Inoculations (tetanus)		○	○	○	○	○
Travel Insurance		●	●	▲	●	●
Driving Licence (national or International Driving Permit)		●	●	●	●	●
Car Insurance Certificate		○	○	●	○	○
Car Registration Document		●	●	●	●	●

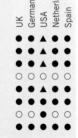

WEBSITES

Further details on attractions, dining, shopping, nightlife and recreation are available from:

www.visitflorida.com
www.orlandoinfo.com/uk
www.go2orlando.com

www.floridakiss.com
www.floridastateparks.org
www.miamiandbeaches.com
www.fla-keys.com
www.gotampa.com
www.disney.go.com
www.universalorlando.com

TOURIST OFFICES AT HOME

In the UK:

Visit Florida
c/o KBCPR
Suite 3, Falmer Court
London Road
Uckfield
East Sussex
TN22 1HN
☎ 01825 763633

In the US:

Visit Florida
661 E Jefferson Street
Suite 300
Tallahassee
FL 32301
☎ 850/488-5607
www.flausa.com

HEALTH INSURANCE

Medical insurance cover of at least $1million unlimited cover is strongly recommended, as medical bills can be astronomical and treatment may be withheld if you have no evidence of means to pay.

TIME DIFFERENCES

GMT	Most of Florida	The Panhandle	Germany	Netherlands	Spain
12 noon	7AM	6AM	1PM	1PM	1PM

Local time in Florida is Eastern Standard Time (GMT –5), with the exception of the Panhandle region, west of the Apalachicola River, which is on Central Standard Time (GMT –6). Daylight saving applies (Apr–Oct).

NATIONAL HOLIDAYS

1 Jan *New Year's Day*

Jan (third Mon) *Martin Luther King Jr. Day*

Feb (third Mon) *President's Day*

Mar/Apr *Good Friday*

May (last Mon) *Memorial Day*

4 July *Independence Day*

Sep (first Mon) *Labor Day*

Oct (second Mon) *Columbus Day*

11 Nov *Veterans' Day*

Nov (fourth Thu) *Thanksgiving*

25 Dec *Christmas Day*

Boxing Day is not a public holiday in the US. Some shops open on National Holidays.

WHAT'S ON WHEN

January *Art Deco Weekend:* Miami's Art Deco district hosts a street festival in mid-January featuring period music, classic automobiles and fashions.

February *Daytona Speed Weeks* (first three weeks): Car racing extravaganza.

Silver Spurs Rodeo (last weekend): Cowboy skills on show in Kissimmee.

March *Annual Sanibel Shell Fair* (first week): Sea shell displays and crafts in America's top shelling spot.

Carnaval Miami (second weekend): The nation's biggest Hispanic festival with top entertainers and parades.

Florida Indian Association Pow Wow (last weekend): The largest Native American "get-together", at Fort Pierce, with singing, dancing and art competitions.

April *Pompano Beach Seafood Festival* (last weekend): Seafood, live music, arts and crafts on the Gold Coast.

Jacksonville Jazz Festival (last weekend): Free festival featuring a host of stars.

May *Florida Folk Festival:* Musicians gather at the Stephen Foster State Cultural Center in White Springs.

SunFest (first week): Florida's premier music, arts and boating celebration in West Palm Beach.

Cajun/Zydeco Crawfish Festival (first weekend): Multiple stages at Fort Lauderdale with live music plus gumbo, crawfish and watermelon to enjoy.

June *Fiesta of Five Flags* (early Jun): Boat and street parades, sandcastle contest and more in Pensacola.

July *Suncoast Offshore Grand Prix* (Jun–Jul): Regatta races, fishing tournaments and entertainment culminating in the race on Sarasota Bay.
Hemingway Days: celebration of the writer and former Key West resident.
Independence Day (Jul 4): Celebrations throughout the state.

August *Venice Seafood Festival*: Seafood cooking competitions and boat exhibitions attract crowds to this beach town.

September *Las Olas Art Fair* (early Sep): Art sales, music and food along Fort Lauderdale's main shopping street.

October *Fantasy Fest* (last week): Key West's Wild Halloween carnival with a distinctly Caribbean twist.

November *Amelia Heritage Festival* (Thanksgiving–New Year): Civil War re-enactments and tours of Fernandina Beach's historic district.

December *Mickey's Very Merry Christmas Party*: Festive celebrations at the Magic Kingdom® in the Walt Disney World® Resort.
Festival of Lights: A spectacular display at Silver Springs (Dec 12–27).

THEME PARK CELEBRATIONS

Public holidays are a great excuse for central Florida's theme parks to break out the fireworks and party hats to celebrate in style. In spring, Universal Studios® hosts a spectacular six-week Mardi Gras (Feb–Mar), and Disney's Magic Kingdom® holds an enormous Easter Sunday Parade.

Fireworks and marching bands accompany the Independence Day celebrations, and the run-up to Halloween is another favorite, with special parties at SeaWorld as well as at Magic Kingdom® and Universal Studios®. A few weeks later all the parks go to town for Christmas and New Year.

© Disney

Getting there

BY AIR

Miami International Airport

10 miles/16km to Miami Beach

N/A

30 minutes

25 minutes

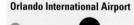

Orlando International Airport

9.25 miles/15km to city center

N/A

45 minutes

30 minutes

Most visitors to Florida arrive at the international airport gateways of Miami and Orlando. Some direct scheduled flights also arrive at Tampa, and charter flights to Sanford (for Orlando), Daytona, Fort Myers and Fort Lauderdale are increasingly popular. US domestic airlines serve numerous local airports.

BY RAIL
See Public Transport ➤ 27.

BY BUS
See Public Transport ➤ 27.

BY CAR
Automobile rental agencies are based at the major airports. but try to book your car in advance. Keep in mind you won't need a car if you plan on simply getting to the town center or resort destination.

The rental agency should provide a local and state map for you, and when you leave the airport you'll find that the greatest distances can be covered by the interstate highway system. I-95 and I-75 skim past Miami; I-75 runs through Tampa; from Tampa, I-4 links to I-95 in Daytona Beach by way of Orlando; and in the panhandle, I-10 links Jacksonville to Tallahassee and Pensacola. FYI: Even-numbered highways go east–west, odd-numbered routes travel north–south.

Getting around

PUBLIC TRANSPORT

Air US domestic carriers serve local airports in all Florida's major cities and vacation destinations. International airports such as Orlando receive direct flights from around 70 different US destinations. Domestic APEX airfares are reasonable and it is worth shopping around for good deals.

Trains Daily Amtrak (☎ 1-800/USA RAIL) services from Washington DC arrive the following day at Orlando (22 hours), Miami (27 hours) and Tampa (28 hours). The overnight AutoTrain service carries cars and passengers from Lorton, VA to Sanford (for Orlando). There is also a triweekly cross-country service from Los Angeles via the Panhandle for Miami. Train services within Florida are very limited; visitors to the southeast can use the inexpensive Tri-Rail commuter network which links Miami and West Palm Beach via Fort Lauderdale and Boca Raton.

Buses Greyhound buses provide a fairly comprehensive network of routes linking Florida's main cities and towns (☎ 1-800 229 9424). Passes for unlimited travel from four to 60 days are best purchased overseas, though savings are available on advance-purchase tickets within the US. Local bus services are infrequent.

Urban transportation Door-to-door airport shuttle bus services to downtown and resort areas are an inexpensive and convenient alternative to taxis. Urban bus routes are generally geared toward commuters, although Orlando is well served by Lynx buses and the I-Ride service along International Drive. In Miami, some Metrobus services can be used for sightseeing; downtown is served by the Metromover light rail link; and there are Metrorail connections to Coconut Grove and Coral Gables.

FARES AND TICKETS

Public transportation tickets are generally about $1. Sometimes transfers are free. If you think you'll be using buses and shuttles frequently, ask about an all-day pass. Also, in Miami, Orlando, and Tampa, the city provides free shuttle services along the most popular tourist routes.

TAXIS

Taxis ("cabs"), can be picked up from the airport or hotel or reserved by telephone (see *Yellow Pages)*. Rates are around $2.80 for the first mile and around $1.50 for each additional mile. Water taxi services are available in Miami, Fort Lauderdale and Jacksonville.

DRIVING

- Speed limit on interstate highways: 55–70mph (88–112kph).
- Speed limit on main roads: 55–65mph (88–104kph).
- Speed limit on urban roads: 20–35mph (32–56kph).
- All speed limits are strictly enforced.
- Seat belts must be worn by drivers and front seat passengers. Car seats are mandatory for under-threes; older children need a safety seat or seat belt.
- There are tough drinking and driving laws. Never drive under the influence of alcohol. Opened cans or bottles containing alcohol in cars are illegal.
- Gasoline (fuel) is cheaper in America than in Europe. It is sold in American gallons (five American gallons equal 18 litres) and comes in three grades, all unleaded. Many gas stations have automatic pumps that accept notes and major credit cards.
- If you break down pull over, raise the hood (bonnet), turn on the hazard lights and call the rental company or the breakdown number (on or near the dashboard). The American Automobile Association (AAA) provides certain reciprocal facilities to affiliated motoring organizations in other countries. For AAA breakdown assistance ☎ 1-800 222 4357 (toll free).

CAR RENTAL

The best way to get around in Florida. Rates are very competitive. Take an unlimited mileage deal, collision damage waiver and adequate (more than minimal) insurance. There is a surcharge on drivers under 25 and the minimum age is often 21 (sometimes 25).

Being there

TOURIST OFFICES

Fort Lauderdale
100 E. Broward, Suite 200
☎ 954/765-4466

Fort Myers (Sanibel and Captiva Islands)
1159 Causeway Boulevard, Sanibel
☎ 239/472-1080

Key West
402 Wall Street
☎ 305/294-2587

Miami
701 Brickell Avenue, Suite 2700
☎ 305/539-3000 and 800/933-8448

Orlando
8723 International Drive, Suite 101
☎ 407/363-5872

Palm Beach
400 Royal Palm Way, Suite 106
☎ 561/655-3282

Pensacola
1401 E. Gregory Street
☎ 850/434-1234

St. Augustine
88 Riberia Street
☎ 904/829-1711

St. Petersburg and Clearwater
13805 58th Street N., Suite 2-200, Clearwater
☎ 727/464-7200

Sarasota
701 N. Tamiami Trail
☎ 941/957-1877

MONEY

An unlimited amount of American dollars can be imported or exported, but amounts of over $10,000 must be reported to US Customs. US traveler's checks are accepted as cash in most places (not taxis) as are credit cards (Amex, Visa, Access, Mastercard, Diners).

Dollar bills come in 1, 2, 5, 10, 20, 50 and 100 denominations. Note that all dollar bills are the same size and color – all greenbacks. One dollar is made up of 100 cents. Coins are of 1 cent (penny), 5 cents (nickel), 10 cents (dime), 25 cents (quarter) and occassionally one dollar coins.

TIPS/GRATUITIES

Yes ✓ No ✗		
It is useful to carry plenty of small notes		
Restaurants (if service not included)	✓	15–20%
Cafeterias/fast-food outlets	✗	
Bar Service	✓	15%
Taxis	✓	15%
Tour guides (discretionary)	✓	
Hotels (chambermaid/doorman etc)	✓	$1 per day
Porters	✓	$1 per bag
Toilets (rest rooms)	✗	

POSTAL AND INTERNET SERVICES

Post offices in Florida are few and far between. Vending machines sell stamps at a 25 percent premium; it is best to purchase them at their face value in your hotel. Post offices are usually open Monday to Friday 9–5; hotels and major attractions often provide postal services.

Internet access is available at internet cafes, hotel rooms and business centers, and other locations such as Kinko's copying centers. Prices vary but are generally inexpensive and are charged by either the hour or half hour in internet cafes. Many hotels and cafes have free WiFi access.

TELEPHONES

Making telephone calls from hotel rooms is expensive. Public telephones are found in hotel lobbies, drugstores, restaurants, gas stations and at the roadside. A local call costs 25 cents. Dial "0" for the operator. To "call collect" means to reverse the charges.

Many tourist offices, hotels, airlines, and car rental companies list toll-free phone numbers. Before dialing their toll number, check to see if there's an alternate '800' number beginning with 1-800, 1-866, 1-877, or 1-888. If you can't find it in the phonebook, call 1-800 5551212 for a voice-prompted directory. It won't cost you a dime.

International dialing codes
From Florida (US) to:
UK: 011 44
Ireland: 011 353

Australia: 011 61
Germany: 011 49
Netherlands: 011 31
Spain: 011 34

Emergency telephone numbers
Police 911
Fire 911
Ambulance 911

EMBASSIES AND CONSULATES

UK 305/374-1522(Miami)
Germany ☎ 305/358-0290 (Miami)
Netherlands ☎ 786/866-0480 (Miami)
Spain ☎ 305/446-5511 (Miami)

HEALTH ADVICE

Sun advice By far the most common cause of ill health among visitors to Florida is too much sun. Use sunscreen on the beach and when sightseeing. Ensure that everyone drinks plenty of fluids. For minor sunburn, aloe vera gel is very soothing.
Drugs Medicines can be bought at drugstores, though certain drugs generally available elsewhere require a prescription in the US. Acetaminophen is the US equivalent of paracetamol. Use an insect repellent containing DEET, and cover up after dark to avoid being bitten by mosquitoes.
Safe water Tap water is drinkable throughout Florida, though not particularly palatable. Mineral water is cheap and readily available. Restaurants usually provide customers with a pitcher of iced tap water.
Dental services Your medical insurance cover should include dental treatment, which is readily available, but expensive. Have a check-up before you go. Dental referral telephone numbers are in the *Yellow Pages* telephone directory or ask at your hotel.

PERSONAL SAFETY

Florida is not generally a dangerous place but to help prevent crime and accidents:

- Never open your hotel room door unless you know who is there. If in doubt call hotel security.
- Always lock your front and/or patio doors when sleeping in the room or going out. Use the safety chain/lock for security.
- When driving keep all car doors locked.

- If lost, stop in a well-lit gas station or ask for directions in a hotel, restaurant or shop.
- Never approach alligators, as they can outrun a man.

ELECTRICITY

Sockets take two-prong, flat-pin plugs. Visitors should bring adaptors for their three-pin and two-round-pin plugs. European visitors should bring a voltage transformer as well as an adapter. The power supply is: 110/120 volts AC (60 cycles).

OPENING HOURS

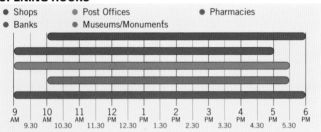

Shopping malls stay open until 9pm or later during the week, and many open on Sundays from around 11–5. Stores in resort areas may also keep more flexible hours. Post offices are not always easy to find and are closed on Saturdays; hotels will often help with basic postal needs. Theme park opening hours vary seasonally. Museum hours also vary; many close on Mondays, but stay open late one night a week. There are 24-hour pharmacies in all major towns; details will be posted at other pharmacies.

LANGUAGE

The official language of the US is English, and, given that one third of all overseas visitors come from the UK, Florida's natives have few problems coping with British accents and dialects. Hotel staff in larger tourist hotels may speak other European languages; Spanish is widely spoken, as many workers in the hotel and catering industries are of Latin American origin. However, many English words have different meanings in the US, opposite are some of the words most likely to cause confusion.

ground floor	*first floor*	rooms with cooking	*efficiencies*
first floor	*second floor*	facilities	
flat	*apartment*	luggage	*baggage*
holiday apartment	*condominium, condo*	hotel porter	*bellhop*
lift	*elevator*	chambermaid	*room maid*
tap	*faucet*	surname	*last name*
cheque	*check*	25 cent coin	*quarter*
traveller's cheque	*traveler's check*	banknote	*bill*
1 cent coin	*penny*	banknote (colloquial)	*greenback*
5 cent coin	*nickel*	dollar (colloquial)	*buck*
10 cent coin	*dime*	cashpoint	*automatic teller*
grilled	*broiled*	biscuit	*cookie*
frankfurter	*hot dog*	scone	*biscuit*
prawn	*shrimp*	sorbet	*sherbet*
aubergine	*eggplant*	jelly	*jello*
courgette	*zucchini*	jam	*jelly*
maize	*corn*	confectionery	*candy*
chips (potato)	*fries*	spirit	*liquor*
crisps (potato)	*chips*	soft drink	*soda*
car	*automobile*	petrol	*gas, gasoline*
bonnet (of car)	*hood*	railway	*railroad*
boot (of car)	*trunk*	tram	*streetcar*
caravan	*trailer*	underground	*subway*
lorry	*truck*	platform	*track*
motorway	*freeway*	single ticket	*one-way ticket*
main road	*highway*	return ticket	*round-trip ticket*
shop	*store*	toilet	*rest room*
chemist (shop)	*drugstore*	trousers	*pants*
bill (in a restaurant)	*check*	nappy	*diaper*
cinema	*movie theater*	glasses	*eyeglasses*
pavement	*sidewalk*	post	*mail*
subway	*underpass*	postcode	*zip code*
gangway	*aisle*	long-distance call	*trunk call*

Best places to see

1 Art Deco District, Miami

Fantastic, funky and fun, Miami Beach's celebrated Art Deco District is a slice of history and one of the hippest spots on the planet.

Hot movie location and fashion shoot backdrop of the 1990s, chic playground of the glitterati from Gloria Estefan to Madonna, the Art Deco District has come a long way from the dingy, run-down neighborhood the City of Miami was anxious to

bulldoze in the 1970s. With a listing on the US National Register of Historic Places and the first 20th-century site to be recognized, the Art Deco District includes 1,200-plus significant buildings in an area running north from 6th Street to 23rd Street, and east–west from Ocean Drive to Lenox Avenue.

Ocean Drive is the epicenter of the neighborhood. This strip of glamorous oceanfront hotels showcases three basic architectural styles: the traditional art deco buildings of the early 1930s; the rounded corners, racy lines and aerodynamic styling of Streamline Moderne; and a selection of classical Mediterranean Revival edifices. A special feature of Miami's art deco style is the frequent use of tropical motifs such as palm trees, exuberant foliage and graceful flamingos. The strikingly bright pastel color schemes are a modern departure designed to highlight these entertaining decorative devices. The **Art Deco Welcome Center** provides maps and details of guided tours. A nighttime visit is highly recommended for the amazing neon lights.

✚ *Miami Beach 3e (Welcome Center)* 🚌 C, H, K
❓ Art Deco Weekend, Jan
Art Deco Welcome Center
✉ 1001 Ocean Drive ☎ 305/531-3484 🕐 Mon–Fri 11–6, Sat 10–10, Sun 11–10 ❓ Self-guided audio tours available daily 10–4. Walking tours Wed, Fri, Sat, Sun 10:30am, Thu 6:30pm. Bicycle tours on the first and third Sun of the month at 10:30am from Miami Beach Bicycle Center (✉ 601 5th Street, reservations ☎ 305/674-0150)

2 Kennedy Space Center

www.kennedyspacecenter.com

**Mission control for the American space
program opens its doors to the public
with a flourish of space hardware,
IMAX movies and tours.**

This top visitor attraction
offers an unrivaled
opportunity to get
behind the scenes of the
space race, take a look
at its history, marvel at
the technology and catch
a glimpse of what may
be in store for
astronauts in the
21st century.

NASA (National
Aeronautics and Space
Administration) first set up a Florida facility in 1958,
at the nearby Cape Canaveral Air Force Station. This
original base for the early Mercury and Gemini
programs and its museum is one of the bus tours
available. The first launch from the Kennedy Space
Center was *Apollo 8* in 1968. A year later *Apollo 11*
put Neil Armstrong on the moon. Today, there are
regular Space Shuttle launches from Launch
Complex 39, which is on the not-to-be-missed
Kennedy Space Center bus tour. This tour also
includes close up views of the landmark VAB
(Vehicle Assembly Building), the giant crawler-

transporters that trundle the Shuttles to the launch pad at a sedate 1mph (1.6kph), the International Space Station and the excellent *Apollo/Saturn V* Center which contains a complete 363ft (109m) *Saturn V* rocket in the main hall and a launch presentation in the Firing Room Theater.

The Visitor Complex contains a number of diversions including the Galaxy Center where the big-screen IMAX cinemas are located. Exhibits include displays of space vehicles, and artifacts from moon dust and model lunar rovers to space suits. Be sure to visit the Rocket Garden, which is filled with a dozen or more rockets from the earliest Mercury missions to the gantry arm which led the *Apollo 11* astronauts to their capsule. The Astronaut Memorial is a large "space mirror" highlighted by the names of those who died in the pursuit of space exploration. Do not miss the daily Astronaut Encounter, a free Q&A session with an actual NASA astronaut.

✚ 17K ✉ SR405, Merritt Island (off US1 N of Cocoa) ☎ 321/449-4444 ⏰ Daily 9–dusk (closes 5:30 in winter) ✋ Very expensive; includes exhibits, bus tour and IMAX show 🍴 Cafés and snack concessions ($) ❓ KSC bus tours throughout the day; check schedules for Cape Canaveral tours

3 Key West

America's southernmost city, Key West lies at the end of the Florida Keys, torn between an agreeable tropical stupor and the demands of tourism.

Venture onto bustling Duval Street, Key West's touristy main drag, or attend the famous nightly sunset celebrations on Mallory Square pier, and the instant impression is of an island city under siege. But step away from the crowds and the quirky capital of the Conch Republic retains a unique charm in its local character and leafy lanes.

In its early days, Key West was a pirates' lair, later settled by wreckers. These 19th-century salvage operators amassed considerable fortunes and built some of the city's finest architecture, including Key West's Oldest House, which is now a rather ramshackle museum. Other fine examples of historic Key West homes are the

lovely **Audubon House,** visited by famous naturalist and painter John James Audubon in 1832, and the **Hemingway House,** where Ernest Hemingway lived and worked in the 1930s.

The most famous Key West wrecker of modern times is Mel Fisher, who spent 15 years locating and salvaging the Spanish galleons *Atocha* and *Santa Maria,* lost off the Keys in 1622. Gold jewelry and other artifacts from the $450 million treasure trove are on display in the fascinating **Mel Fisher Maritime Heritage Society Museum.** Nearby, the Key West Aquarium reveals underwater mysteries of a different order, including brilliantly colored tropical fish, sharks and sea turtles.

For the best view of Key West, climb the 110ft (33.5m) Key West Lighthouse. The huge lens is still in working order, and there is a museum laid out in the former keeper's quarters. Another worthwhile stop is the East Martello Museum, which combines local history exhibits with an art gallery.

✚ 15T ❷ Conch Republic Celebration, Apr–May; Hemingway Days, Jul

ℹ️ Key West Welcome Center, 38 N. Roosevelt Boulevard

☎ 305/296-4444; www.keywestwelcomecenter.com

Aubudon House

✉ 205 Whitehead Street ☎ 305/294-2116; www.audubonhouse.com ⏰ Daily 9:30–5 💰 Moderate

Hemingway House

✉ 907 Whitehead Street ☎ 305/294-1136; www.hemingwayhome.com ⏰ Daily 9–5 💰 Moderate

Mel Fisher Maritime Heritage Society Museum

✉ 200 Greene Street ☎ 305/294-2633; www.melfisher.org ⏰ Daily 9:30–5 💰 Moderate

4 National Museum of Naval Aviation

www.naval-air.org

This state-of-the-art aviation museum combines top gun fun with a fascinating insight into the history of flight.

More than 170 aircraft and space capsules have been packed into the cavernous halls of this vast museum, laid out in the historic Pensacola Naval Air Station. A glass atrium is big enough to hold four A-4 Skyhawk jets, once flown by the US Navy's Blue Angels display team and now suspended from the roof in flying formation, a full-size re-creation of a World War II aircraft carrier flight deck, complete with a line-up of fighter planes, and numerous "hands-on" simulators and interactive displays.

The guided tours are a highlight. Although all the exhibits are accompanied by storyboards, the tours, led by volunteers who are often veteran pilots, add an unbeatable insider view. They can also point out some of the exhibits it would be easy to miss, such as trainee World War II pilot George Bush's

logbook, a little slice of history from long before he rose to become America's President and Commander-in-Chief. Several of the museum's larger exhibits are parked out on the runway and open to inspection. Spanish colonists first

occupied the site of Fort Barrancas, overlooking
Pensacola Bay, in 1698, and it attracted the
attentions of the US Army during the 1840s.
Tours of the fort and other
areas may be canceled
without notice.

✚ 2C ✉ 750 Radford Drive,
Pensacola Naval Air Station
☎ 850/453-2389 or 1-800
327 5002 🕐 Daily 9–5
✋ Free. Charge for IMAX
cinema and flight simulator
🍴 Café ($) ❓ Guided tours
on request

5 Palm Beach

A fortuitous shipwreck sowed the seeds for Palm Beach, and railroad baron Henry Flagler provided that little extra something – money.

In 1878, a cargo of 20,000 coconuts washed up on Palm Beach and obligingly sprouted into an idyllic tropical backdrop for one of Henry Flagler's splendid resorts. Architect Addison Mizner was equally charmed by his surroundings in the 1920s, and launched a welter of Mediterranean Revival designs that helped shape the style of Florida's most exclusive seaside community. Today, Palm Beach is a millionaires' playground of luxurious mansions, manicured lawns and black-belt shopping, where the smell of money is palpable. For around nine

months of the year things are relatively quiet, but Palm Beach's winter social season is in a class of its own as old money, new money, players and playboys descend for an orgy of parties, polo and charity balls.

Despite the exaggerated country-club atmosphere, tourists are welcome. The 4.5-mile (7-km) Palm Beach Bicycle Trail covers the local highlights, including the **Flagler Museum** in Whitehall, Henry Flagler's sumptuous Palm Beach residence. There are tours of the lavishly furnished 55-room mansion crammed with French, Italian and English antiques, and the private railway carriage in the grounds is a miniature work of art. A hidden treat along the route are the lovely Cluett Memorial Gardens behind the Episcopal Church of Bethesda-by-the-Sea.

The twin poles of Palm Beach's social whirl are the glorious Breakers Hotel and the elegant shopping enclave of Worth Avenue, nicknamed "Fifth Avenue South" for its dazzling collection of designer boutiques and upscale jewelry stores (▶ 70). Tucked away behind the main thoroughfare is a maze of delightful little Addison Mizner-designed courtyards containing smaller shops, galleries and cafés.

➕ 18P
ℹ️ 45 Coconut Row
Flagler Museum
✉️ 1 Whitehall Way ☎ 561/655-2833; www.flagler.org 🕐 Tue–Sat 10–5, Sun 12–5 ♿ Moderate

6 St. Augustine

The oldest continuously inhabited European settlement in the US, St. Augustine predates the arrival of the Pilgrim Fathers by half a century.

Though several attempts were made to establish a foothold in Florida earlier in the 16th century, St. Augustine was founded in 1565 by Pedro Menéndez de Avilés, the newly appointed governor of Florida dispatched by Philip II of Spain to rout the fledgling French colony at Fort Caroline (➤ 165).

St. Augustine is a delight and small enough to explore on foot, though there are mini sightseeing trains and horse-and-carriage rides from Avenida Menendez, north of the Bridge of Lions. The original settlement was razed to the ground by Sir Francis Drake in 1586, but it was rebuilt in the shadow of the **Castillo de San Marcos,** an imposing star-shaped fortress built of limestone from Anastasia Island across the bay. The Spanish garrison lived with their families in the town and one of their homes, the Oldest House, has been restored. Each room is furnished to depict a different period in its remarkable history.

Henry Flagler, the railroad tycoon who helped transform St. Augustine – and Florida's east coast – into a resort destination, honeymooned here in 1883, heralding St. Augustine's Gilded Age. One of Flagler's former hotels, the Alcazar, now houses the Lightner Museum with its fabulous collections of fine and decorative arts dating from this period. Since then the city has added all

manner of museums and historic "experiences" – see the St. Augustine walk (➤ 68–69).

✚ 12E ❓ Arts and Crafts Festival, Mar; Founding Anniversary, Sep
ℹ 10 Castillo Drive ☎ 904/825-1000; www.oldcity.com
Castillo de San Marcos
✉ 1 Castillo Drive ☎ 904/829-6506 🕐 Daily 8:45–4:45
💵 Moderate ❓ Regular tours

7 St. Petersburg

A trio of world-class art museums have transformed sunny St. Petersburg into a leading cultural hot spot.

Once regarded as the Gulf Coast's chief roost for elderly "snowbirds," or winter visitors, St. Petersburg has updated its image considerably in recent years. St. Pete (as it is familiarly known) is the cultural center of the Pinellas Suncoast resort area (▶ 133) a 30-minute drive away.

The grid of broad and tree-shaded downtown streets leads down to Tampa Bay and a causeway anchoring The Pier shopping, dining and entertainment complex to the mainland. Just to the north of here is the **Museum of Fine Arts** housed in an attractive Mediterranean-style villa. The collections start with ancient Greek and Roman sculpture, then move through the major periods of European art to 19th- and 20th-century American works. Asian, African, pre-Columbian and Native American arts and crafts are also well represented.

A few blocks away, the **Florida International Museum** has hosted exhibits on RMS *Titanic*, JFK, Alexander the Great and ancient Egypt. The musuem is affiliated with the Smithsonian Institution and houses artifacts from its collection as well as presenting traveling exhibitions.

The **Salvador Dalí Museum** houses the largest collection of the Surrealist artist's work outside Spain. The guided tours are excellent, and the imaginative gift shop does the artist proud.

✚ 13M

Museum of Fine Arts

✉ 255 Beach Drive ☎ 727/896-2667; www.fine-arts.org
🕐 Tue–Sat 10–5, Sun 1–5 ✋ Moderate

Florida International Museum

✉ 244 Second Avenue N. ☎ 727/341-7900;
www.floridamuseum.org 🕐 Tue–Sat 10–5, Sun noon–5
✋ Expensive

Salvador Dalí Museum

✉ 1000 3rd Street S. ☎ 727/823-3767 🕐 Mon–Sat
9:30–5:30 (8pm Thu), Sun 12–5:30 ✋ Moderate

8 Sanibel & Captiva Islands

A brace of lovely barrier islands linked to the mainland by a causeway, Sanibel and Captiva are havens for shell collectors and beach lovers.

According to local legend, 18th-century pirate José Gaspar once stowed his female captives on these lush islands, famous for their pristine, soft sandy beaches and relaxing atmosphere. Vacationers looking for an action-packed time should avoid Sanibel and Captiva, though there are plenty of sightseeing opportunities across the causeway in Fort Myers (➤ 105–106). The twin islands were swamped by Hurricane Charley in August 2004, and both lost much of their trees and foliage. Nature has a way of repairing itself, and much of the devastation has been concealed. That said, it's a luxury to laze in the sun. If you absolutely have to do something, activities include fishing, golfing, bicycle paths and boat trips from marinas, where it is also possible to rent sailboats and canoes.

The famous beaches are on the Gulf side and they are liberally sprinkled with a fantastic variety of seashells, from the common whelk to speckled junonias and more exotic finds. The best time to look is at low tide or after a storm, but be warned: live shelling is illegal and punishable by jail and a fine. Amateur shell collectors and full-blown conchologists alike should take the time to visit the **Bailey-Matthews Shell Museum,** which fields exhibits on shell lore and arts as well as collections of shells from around the world.

The other "must-see" attraction on the islands is the **J. N. "Ding" Darling National Wildlife Refuge,** a 5,600-acre (2.240ha) wetlands preserve with a 5-mile (8-km) self-guided wildlife drive (there are excellent narrated tram tours in winter), walking paths and canoe trails. Resident wildlife to look out for includes alligators, osprey, roseate spoonbills and hawks. The drive is best at low tide first thing in the morning or in the evening when the wading birds are feeding (tickets are valid all day).

✚ 14P 🛈 Sanibel Shell Fair, Mar
🛈 1159 Causeway Boulevard, Sanibel ☎ 239/472-1080
Bailey-Matthews Shell Museum
✉ 3075 Sanibel-Captiva Road, Sanibel ☎ 239/395-2233; www.shellmuseum.org 🕐 Daily 10–4 🖐 Inexpensive
J. N. "Ding" Darling National Wildlife Refuge
✉ Sanibel-Captiva Road ☎ 239/472-1100 🕐 Refuge: Sun–Thu 7:30am to dusk. Visitor Center: Nov– Apr Sun–Thu 9–5; May–Oct 9–4 🖐 Refuge: inexpensive. Visitor Center: free

Sarasota

Sarasota's lively cultural scene owes much to circus impresario John Ringling, who created a waterfront estate to house his art collections.

An appealing, small-scale waterfront city combining a handful of diverse sightseeing attractions, easy access to the Tampa Bay area, superb barrier island beaches, and an calendar of performing arts events, Sarasota makes an excellent vacation base.

The city's crown jewel is the **Ringling Museum of Art,** a 66-acre (26.5ha) bayfront spread incorporating John Ringling's magnificent 1920s Venetian-style winter residence Cà d'Zan ("House of John"), a museum of baroque and Renaissance art, and a circus museum full of colorful and curious memorabilia. The beautifully restored 18th-century, 300-seat Asolo Theater may also be open to view.

By the waterfront, the gorgeous Marie Selby Gardens are a feast for the eye, planted with colorful hibiscus, cacti, bromeliads and bamboos. The orchid collection is renowned and there is a tropical foods section, as well as a butterfly garden and displays of botanical illustrations.

John Ringling employed circus elephants to help build the causeway across to St. Armand's Key, and designed St. Armand's Circle, Sarasota's most exclusive shopping enclave. To the south, Lido Key is a popular resort area offering family beaches and water sports. There are public access footpaths to the beaches of Longboat Key, and a popular attraction here is the Mote Aquarium. A research and educational facility, the Mote's centerpiece is a huge shark tank. Other diversions include rescued sea turtles and manatees and touch tanks stocked with crabs and rays. The pelican sanctuary across the parking lot is also well worth a visit.

➕ 14M ❓ Sarasota Jazz Festival, Mar; Music Festival, Jun
ℹ️ 655 N. Tamiami Trail ☎ 941/957-1887 or 1-800 552 9999
Ringling Museum of Art
✉️ 5401 Bayshore Road/US41 ☎ 941/359-5700;
www.ringling.org/musuem_art.asp ⏰ Daily 10–5:30
✋ Moderate

10 Walt Disney World® Resort: Magic Kingdom®

http://disneyworld.disney.go.com

The biggest thing to hit Florida tourism since the railroad, Walt Disney World® continues to set the standard for theme parks worldwide.

Animator and entrepreneur Walt Disney opened his first theme park in California in 1955. Disneyland was an immediate success, but Disney loathed the commercial sprawl that sprang up around the site and resolved to control every aspect of his next venture. In the early 1960s, he secretly amassed a vast land holding outside Orlando, and the Magic Kingdom®, the first phase of the resort, opened in 1971, to be followed by Epcot®, Disney's Hollywood Studios (formerly Disney-MGM Studios) and the blockbuster, Disney's Animal Kingdom® (➤ 143–144).

Based on the original Disneyland prototype, the Magic Kingdom® is Disney's most popular Florida park and should not be missed. Its seven themed lands radiate from the fairytale Cinderella Castle, each providing an imaginative selection of rides and shows. In Adventureland®, there are rip-roaring adventures with the Pirates of the Caribbean and a steamy Jungle Cruise. The Big Thunder Mountain Railroad rollercoaster and Splash Mountain® flume ride are highlights of Wild West-themed Frontierland®. Riverboat rides depart from the

© Disney

© Disney

Liberty Square colonial quarter, which is also home to the entertaining Haunted Mansion and educational Hall of the Presidents, which delivers a potted history of the US through the mouths of former presidents. Mickey's Toontown Fair and Fantasyland are the little children's favorite lands, hosting best-loved cartoon characters and specially scaled down rides. In Tomorrowland® old favorites such as the excellent Space Mountain® rollercoaster has been joined by the Monsters Inc. Comedy Club, a fast-paced and funny improv show where the audience interacts in real time with cartoon characters on a huge movie screen. Next door, Buzz Lightyear's Space Ranger Spin features a laser shoot-out against the evil Zurg.

🕂 15K ⊠ Lake Buena Vista (20 miles/32km south of Orlando) ☎ Information: 407/939-4636; reservations: 407/934-7639 🕓 Check current schedules online 🖐 Very expensive 🍴 A good choice. Make reservations at Guest Relations for table service restaurants ($$–$$$) 🚌 Free shuttle bus from many hotels ❓ Daily parades, shows and nighttime fireworks and laser displays

Best things to do

Good places to have lunch

♛♛ Bahama Breeze ($$)

One of the few places on I-Drive where you can eat outside on the deck. Tasty Mexican, Cuban and Thai dishes share the menu with American meat and seafood options. Enjoy live reggae and Caribbean music nightly.

✉ 8849 International Drive, Orlando ☎ 407/248-2499; www.bahamabreeze.com ⏰ Lunch and dinner

The Bubble Room ($$–$$$)

A festive, toy-filled restaurant in an island paradise sets the perfect tone for perfect dishes including decadent mile-high desserts.

✉ 15001 Captiva Drive, Captiva ☎ 239/472-5558; www.bubbleroomrestaurant.com ⏰ Mon–Thu 4–10, Fri–Sat 4–11, Sun 11–9

♛♛ Buca di Beppo ($$–$$$)

Huge sharable platters of Italian dishes, including a good selection of pasta and pizzas, that would stagger Homer Simpson.

✉ 11511 N. Dale Mabry Highway, Tampa ☎ 813/962-6673; www.bucadibeppo.com ⏰ Lunch and dinner

♛ Crispers ($)

Quick and healthy dishes – nearly all are healthy, taste great and cost under 10 bucks. Try the Citrus Chicken wrap with pineapple, mandarin oranges and sugar walnuts; the margherita flatbread pizza; and the fabulous strawberry-banana smoothie.

✉ 4509 St. John's Avenue, Jacksonville ☎ 904/389-9075; www.crispers.com ⏰ Lunch and dinner

♛♛ ♛♛ Mark's at the Park ($$–$$$)

Mark Militello is one of South Florida's most creative and successful chefs so don't miss the opportunity to sample his Floribbean/Mediterranean cooking.

✉ 344 Plaza Real, Mizner Park, Boca Ranton ☎ 561/395-0770; www.chefmark.com ⏰ Lunch and dinner

💎💎 The Moon Under Water ($$)

Near The Pier and St. Pete's museums and nightlife is this tribute to the glory days of the British Empire; a combination pub and restaurant that serves hand-drawn beers and ales as well as Indian curries, shepherd's pie and fish and chips.

✉ 332 Beach Drive N.E., St. Petersburg ☎ 727/896-6160 🕐 Lunch and dinner

💎💎 News Café ($)

You'll think you're on the Riviera when you dine at this sidewalk café across from the Atlantic Ocean. Miami beach trendies share tables with tourists as they enjoy a sunrise breakfast, sandwiches and dinners watching the parade of people passing by. Also at 2901 Florida Avenue, Coconut Grove (☎ 305/774 6397).

✉ 800 Ocean Drive, Miami Beach ☎ 305/538-6397; www.newscafe.com 🕐 24 hours

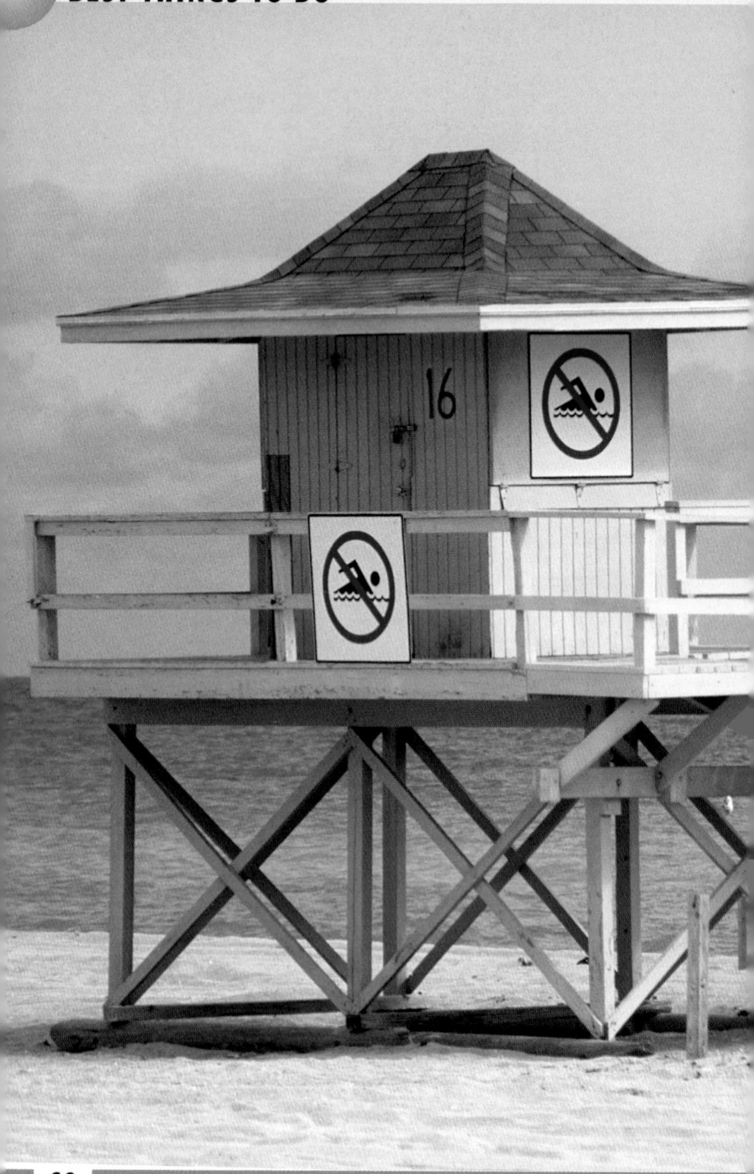
16

Top beaches

Alternative attractions

Florida's big-name theme parks are the obvious choice for entertaining the children but should you want a different day out then try some of the following:

SOUTH FLORIDA AND THE KEYS
Butterfly World
Thousands of brightly colored butterflies flutter about the giant tropical aviaries at this popular attraction.

✉ 3600 W. Sample Road (I-95/Exit 36), Coconut Creek, Fort Lauderdale
☎ 954/977-4434; www.butterflyworld.com 🕐 Mon–Sat 9–5, Sun 11–5

Teddy Bear Museum
Over 3,000 toy and ornamental bears of all sizes and descriptions inhabit this cutesy museum in the woods.

✉ 2511 Pine Ridge Road, Naples ☎ 239/598-2711 🕐 Tue–Sat 10–5

CENTRAL FLORIDA
Green Meadows Petting Farm
In a shady farmyard setting youngsters can experience animal encounters with calves, lambs, ducklings and ponies.

✉ 1368 S Poinciana Boulevard, Kissimmee ☎ 407/846-0770;
www.greenmeadowsfarm.com 🕐 Daily 9:30–4

Wet 'n Wild
Watery fun at the best water park in the area outside Walt Disney World® Resort. Kiddie pools and sunbathing decks.

✉ 6200 International Drive, Orlando ☎ 407/351-1800 or 1-800 992-9453;
www.wetnwildorlando.com 🕐 Daily from 9am in summer, 10am in winter

US Astronaut Hall of Fame
Along from the Kennedy Space Center (➤ 38–39), the Hall of Fame offers an exciting and accessible array of space exhibits.

✉ 6225 Vectorspace Boulevard/SR405, Titusville ☎ 321/867-5000
🕐 Daily 9–5

NORTH FLORIDA
Adventure Landing
A pirate-themed summer-season water park is the main attraction. Children can also let swing in the baseball batting cages, play miniature golf and race go-carts.

✉ 4825 Blanding Boulevard, Jacksonville ☎ 904/771-2804; www.adventurelanding.com

🕐 Mon–Fri 10–10, Sat, Sun 10–midnight

Junior Museum of Bay County
A low-key attraction for younger children, this small museum adopts a "hands-on" approach to science, art and nature exhibits.

✉ 1731 Jenks Avenue, Panama City ☎ 850/769-6128; www.jrmuseum.org

🕐 Mon–Fri 9–4:30, Sat 10–4

Shipwreck Island Water Park
Enjoy 6-acres (2.5 ha) of watery thrills and spills, lazy inner tube rides and speed slides. Little children are kept busy in the Tadpole Hole play area, and there are sunbathing decks and restaurants.

✉ 12000 Front Beach Road ☎ 850/234-0368; www.shipwreckisland.com

🕐 Jun–Labor Day 10:30–5:30; Apr–May, Sep reduced hours. Closed Oct–Mar

St. Augustine Alligator Farm and Zoological Park
When the children have had their fill of St. Augustine's history, cross the bay to Anastasia Island and take them to the World's Original Alligator Farm founded in 1893. There are 23 species of crocodilians, plus bird shows and farm animals in the petting zoo.

✉ 999 Anastasia Boulevard (A1A), St. Augustine ☎ 904/824-3337; www.alligatorfarm.com 🕐 Daily 9–5

Best places to stay

MIAMI
◆◆◆ Biltmore Hotel ($$$)
The luxurious 1920s Mediterranean Revival-style landmark has grand public rooms and spacious accommodations. There is an excellent restaurant; a magnificent outdoor swimming pool, tennis and golf.
✉ 1200 Anastasia Avenue, Coral Gables, Miami ☎ 305/445-1926 or 1-800 727 1926; www.biltmorehotel.com

◆◆ Miami River Inn ($$)
A lovely 40-room hotel in Little Havana with lots of character, including hardwood floors and antique-furnished rooms. There's an outdoor pool and spa tub.
✉ 118 SW South River Drive, Miami ☎ 305/305-0045 or 1-800 468 3589; www.miamiriverinn.com

SOUTH FLORIDA AND THE KEYS
◆◆◆◆ The Breakers ($$$)
Palatial hotel originally built by Henry Flagler in 1896, but rebuilt in 1925 after a fire. It offers the ultimate luxury and unparalleled service.
✉ 1 S. County Road, Palm Beach ☎ 561/655-6611 or 1-888 273 2537

◆◆◆◆ Marina Del Mar Resort and Marina ($–$$$)
All kinds of water-based fun, including diving, boat rentals, fishing and swimming with dolphins. All rooms have balconies with marina views.
✉ 527 Caribbean Drive, Key Largo ☎ 305/451-4107 or 1-800 451 3483

◆◆◆ South Seas Island Resort ($$$)
Large, attractively landscaped resort with hotel rooms, condos and cottages, beach, pools and marina.
✉ 5400 Plantation Road, Captiva ☎ 239/472-5111 or 1-800 449 1827

CENTRAL FLORIDA
☜☜ Disney's All-Star Sports, Movie and Music Resorts ($–$$)
Three good-value theme resorts with sporting, movie and musical motifs. Handy in-room pizza deilvery; great after a day at the parks.

✉ 1701–1991 W. Buena Vista Lake Drive, Walt Disney World® Resort

☎ All-Star Sports: 407/939-5000; All-Star Music: 407/939 6000; reservations: 407/934 7639

☜☜☜☜ Hard Rock Hotel ($$$)
The rock themed hotel/café chain worked with Universal to create this huge complex. Walking distance from the two theme parks.

✉ 5800 Universal Boulevard, Orlando ☎ 407/503-2000

☜☜☜ Quality Suites Maingate East ($$)
Good family hotel with one- or two-bedroom suites with kitchens around a quadrangle with a pool. Continental breakfast and Disney shuttle included. In walking distance of Old Town entertainment/ shopping complex.

✉ 5876 Irlo Bronson Memorial Highway, Kissimmee

☎ 407/396-804

NORTH FLORIDA
☜☜☜ Coombs House Inn ($–$$)
Lovely Victorian bed-and-breakfast in a grand old home furnished with antiques and within walking distance of restaurants and stores. Some rooms are located in a cottage across the street.

✉ 80 6th Street, Apalachocola ☎ 850/653-9199

Governor's Inn ($$–$$$)
Only a few blocks from the capitol buildings, this converted warehouse is now a 41-room boutique hotel. Soft beds, cozy rooms and a complimentary Continental breakfast each morning.

✉ 209 S. Adams Street, Tallahassee ☎ 850/681-6855; thegovinn.com

Top outdoor activities

Birdwatching: Corkscrew Swamp Sanctuary (➤ 98), Merritt Island National Wildlife Refuge and the Florida Keys are among the top spots.

Boat trips: Notable boating areas include the Lee Island Coast, the Everglades (➤ 98–99) and the Keys (➤ 108–111).

Canoeing: Many riverfront state parks provide canoe trails.

Diving: Coral reef diving in the Keys (➤ 108) and fascinating wreck sites off the Emerald Coast.

Fishing: Licenses are required for fishing, bait and tackle shops can assist in obtaining the correct ones.

Golf: Florida is one of the world's top golfing destinations with over 1,000 golf courses around the state.

Motorsports: Major events at Daytona International Speedway (▶ 156), and Homestead-Miami Speedway.

Polo: The sport of kings is a top winter pursuit on the Gold Coast.

Tennis: There are numerous hotel and public tennis courts.

Water sports: Hotels and beachfront concessions rent out windsurfing, sailing, kayaking and dive equipment.

a walk around St. Augustine

The compact historic heart of St. Augustine (► 46–47) is the ideal size to explore on foot. This short walk starts from the 18th-century City Gates at the north end of St. George Street.

Lined with historic buildings, stores and restaurants, St. George Street is the old city's main thoroughfare, now a pedestrian mall. Here the Oldest Wooden Schoolhouse (No. 14) dates from around 1788, and the fascinating **Colonial Spanish Quarter** (No. 33) depicts life in the 18th-century colonial town with the help of reconstructed buildings and a working blacksmith's shop. Peña-Peck House (No. 143) was originally built for the Spanish Royal

Treasurer in the 1740s, but it has been restored and furnished in mid-19th century style.

At Plaza de la Constitucion, cut diagonally across to the right and take King Street. Cross Cordova Street.

On the right, Flagler College was once the grand Ponce de Leon Hotel, opened in 1888. Visitors are free to enter the lobby and peek into the elaborate Rotunda dining room.

Return to the Plaza and walk down the south side. Turn right on Aviles Street.

The Spanish Military Hospital (No. 3) takes an unsentimental look at 18th-century medical practices.

Detour down Artillery Lane (right) for the Oldest Store Museum, or continue down Aviles Street to No. 20.

The 1797 Ximenez-Fatio House was turned into a boarding house in the 1830s. It has been cleverly restored and each room is furnished in the appropriate style for a variety of 19th-century lodgers from a military man to a lady invalid.

Continue along Aviles. Turn left on Bridge Street, right on Charlotte Street, and left on St. Francis Street for the Oldest House (➤ 46).

Distance 1 mile (1.6 km)
Time 4 hours with stops
Start point City Gates, S. George Street
End point Oldest House, St. Francis Street
Lunch Florida Cracker Café ($–$$) ✉ 81 St. George Street
☎ 904/829-0397

Great shopping

MIAMI
Lincoln Road Mall, Miami Beach
On this buzzing pedestrian street you'll find an entertaining mixture of art galleries, boutiques and specialty stores from designer lighting emporiums to hand-rolled cigars.

✉ 924 Lincoln Road, Miami Beach ☎ 305/531-3442

SOUTH FLORIDA AND THE KEYS
Duval and Simonton Streets, Key West
While Duval is Key West's busiest shopping street, there are a couple of factory stores on Simonton. Check out the tropical prints at Key West Fabrics and Fashions (No. 201); and the designs at The T-Shirt Factory (No. 316).

Las Olas Boulevard, Fort Lauderdale
This attractive downtown shopping street is well stocked with boutiques and galleries. The new Las Olas Riverfront complex overlooks the New River.

✉ Las Olas Boulevard, Fort Lauderdale; www.lasolasboulevard.com

Third Street South and the Avenues, Naples
This charming small shopping and dining enclave offers a tempting selection of contemporary fashion, galleries and specialty shops.

✉ 3rd Street S. (between Broad and 14th Avenues S), Naples
☎ 239/649-6707

Worth Avenue, Palm Beach
Small but perfectly formed, and great for window-shopping, the upscale shopping enclave of Worth Avenue comprises four gracious little blocks lined with

a collection expensive designer boutiques.

✉ Worth Avenue (between S Ocean Boulevard and Coconut Row); www.worth-avenue.com

CENTRAL FLORIDA

Downtown Disney® Marketplace

Home to a selection of souvenir and gift shops, but most importantly the vast and dangerously tempting World of Disney.

✉ Buena Vista Drive, Lake Buena Vista, Walt Disney World® Resort ☎ 407/828-3058

Historic Cocoa Village

In this quiet little corner of old Cocoa you'll find an appealing selection of craft shops, gift stores, boutiques and cafés laid out along shady lanes.

✉ Brevard Avenue (South of SR520), Cocoa Beach
☎ 321/631-9075

Mall at Millenia

The most up-market mall in Orlando with Macy's and Bloomingdales department stores.

✉ 4200 Conroy Road, Orlando ☎ 407/363-3555

Park Avenue, Orlando

Winter Park offers a relaxing alternative to the big shopping malls, it's great place for browsing.

✉ Park Avenue at New York Avenue, Orlando ☎ 407/644-8281; www.parkave-winterpark.com

St. Armands Circle, Sarasota

Downtown has The Quay mall, but St. Armands Circle's specialty stores are more tempting.

✉ St. Armands Key (SR789), Sarasota ☎ 941/388-1554

Exploring

Big, brash, and sexy, Miami comes on like a Hollywood starlet displaying her attractions in an enviable tropical setting. The palm trees, the shimmering beaches, the wide blue skies, and the sailboats skimming across glittering Biscayne Bay are just as they should be. The vertiginous downtown skyline serves the joint purpose of sightseeing attraction and a measure of the city's recent success. This is a city on the make and it does not care who knows.

Miami has an intriguingly international flavor. Poised at the gateway to Latin America, there is a touch of salsa in its soul and a large and voluble Cuban community who know how to make good coffee and dine late. Europeans have also made inroads, particularly in SoBe (South Beach), the terminally hip Miami Beach Art Deco District, whose unique brand of cutting-edge kitsch has become an style icon.

Miami

**It is little more than a century since
pioneer Julia Tuttle lured Henry Flagler
and his railroad south with a bouquet
of orange blossom despatched during the devastating
1894–95 Great Freeze in central Florida. Today, the
sprawling bayfront metropolis has a population of
2.2 million and ranks as the third most popular city
destination in the US after Los Angeles and New York.**

The main resort areas are on Miami Beach, with the Art Deco
District in the south, the major hotels in the middle, and more
budget-oriented options in the north. On the mainland, downtown
is well supplied with executive-style hotels, there are a few
upscale choices in Coconut Grove and Coral Lakes, or smart
resorts on Key Biscayne, and budget places near the airport.
Miami's sights are widespread, with several family attractions a
good 45-minute drive south of downtown. To get the most from
a stay of more than a couple of days, a car is helpful.

ART DECO DISTRICT

Best places to see, ➤ 36–37.

BASS MUSEUM OF ART

Tucked away in a small grassy park, the Bass is a real treat laid out over two floors of a 1930 art deco building. European old master paintings, drawings, and sculpture from the Renaissance, baroque and rococo periods are augmented by a superb collection of 16th-century Flemish tapestries. There are more modern works and collections of antique furniture and *objets d'art*. As well as the permanent collections the museum hosts a broad-ranging program of visiting exhibitions and weekend cultural events.

www.bassmuseum.org

➕ *Miami Beach 3c* ✉ 2121 Park Avenue, Miami Beach ☎ 305/673-7530 ⏰ Tue–Sat 10–5, Sun 11–5 ✋ Moderate

BAYSIDE MARKETPLACE

A waterfront shopping, dining, and entertainment complex, downtown Bayside is a popular stop on the tourist trail. The open-air mall has around 150 boutiques and gift stores, cafés, bars and restaurants. Free entertainment is provided by street performers and there is live music nightly. Regular Biscayne Bay sightseeing cruises depart from the dock.

www.baysidemarketplace.com

➕ *Downtown Miami 4c* ✉ 401 N. Biscayne Boulevard ☎ 305/577-3344 ⏰ Mon–Thu 10–10, Fri–Sat 10–11, Sun 11–9 🚉 College/Bayside 🚌 C, S, 16, 48, 95

COCONUT GROVE

The Grove is one of Miami's oldest and most appealing neighborhoods. Once a byword for bohemian living, the area has seen an influx of bright young things, and the busy intersection of Grand Avenue and Main Highway is now crowded with sidewalk cafés, chic shops and galleries and is home to the CocoWalk shopping center (➤ 91). However, it is still a great place to hang out. There are historic homes in the pioneer **Barnacle State Historic Site,** hidden in a hardwood hammock on the water, and palatial Vizcaya (➤ 86). Visit the 1920s Coconut Grove Playhouse for its elaborate Spanish-style stucco facade and reputation as a leading local repertory theater.

www.coconutgrove.com

🚏 *Downtown Miami 3f (off map)* 🚌 12, 24, 48 ❓ Goombay Festival, Jun

Barnacle State Historic Site

✉ 3485 Main Highway ☎ 305/448-9445 🕐 Fri–Mon 9–4. Tours at 10, 11:30, 1, 2:30. Tue–Thu group tours by appointment 💷 Inexpensive

a walk around South Beach

This walk starts at the Art Deco Welcome Center (► 37), and heads north on Ocean Drive to 15th Street, past an array of delectable deco delights.

Turn left on 15th, left on Collins Avenue, doubling back for 200yds (183m) to a right turn onto Española Way.

A pretty little Mediterranean pastiche, between Drexel and Washington avenues, Espanola is a good place to stop for coffee and window-shopping.

Continue westward on Espanola Way to Pennsylvania Avenue. Turn right and head north to Lincoln Road; turn left.

Dozens of galleries, boutiques and café-restaurants have gravitated to the pedestrian-zoned Lincoln Road Mall. Art

deco highlights include the restored Lincoln Theatre and the Sterling Building with its glass-block headband (spectacular at night). The wonderful sidewalk eatery, Van Dyke Café, is in the 800 block.

Head north on Meridian Avenue for three-and-a-half blocks to the Holocaust Memorial.

The centerpiece of this moving memorial is a giant bronze arm reaching skyward from a seething mass of doomed humanity. Victims' names are inscribed on a memorial wall and the horror of the Holocaust is described in words and pictures.

Double back to 19th Street and turn left alongside the Convention Center parking lot. At the end of the street turn left and look for the canal-side footpath on the right, which rejoins Washington Avenue. Cross Washington on to 21st Street. After a block-and-a-half, the Bass Museum of Art (► 76) will be found on the left. Turn right along Collins Avenue, and head south, back toward Ocean Drive and the Art Deco Welcome Center, passing on the way some of Miami Beach's finest hotels.

Distance Just over 2.5 miles (4km) to Bass Museum of Art; 4-mile (6.5km) circuit to Art Deco Welcome Center
Time 2 hours with coffee stops and browsing. Add at least an hour for a visit to the museum **Start/end point** Art Deco Welcome Center ✚ Miami Beach 3e 🚌 K, S, M, C **Lunch** Van Dyke Café ($) ✉ 846 Lincoln Road ☎ 305/534-3600

CORAL GABLES

A gracious product of the 1920s land boom, the leafy residential enclave of Coral Gables is deemed grand enough to have its own driving tour. Maps are available from City Hall, on Miracle Mile, and stops along the way include the fabulous Biltmore Hotel (▶ 87) and developer George Merrick's bijou "Villages." These little groups of homes were built in a variety of eye-catching architectural styles, from Chinese to Dutch Colonial.

 17R 🚌 24, 72

FAIRCHILD TROPICAL GARDEN

These magnificent botanical gardens, the largest in the US, consist of an 83-acre (33ha) tract of lawns and lakes, hardwood hammocks and miniature rain forest. The palm collection is one of the largest in the world, and there are tropical blooms and a specialist Rare Plant House. A narrated streetcar tour sets the scene; then you are on your own to explore the trails through coastal mangrove and Everglades areas. Next to the Fairchild, Matheson Hammock

Park is a good place to swim and enjoy a picnic.

www.fairchildgarden.org

➕ 17R ✉ 10901 Old Cutler Road, Coral Gables

☎ 305/667-1651 🕐 Daily 9:30–4:30

✋ Moderate 🍴 Café ($) 🚌 65

KEY BISCAYNE

Reached by the Rickenbacker Causeway (toll), which affords a fantastic view of downtown Miami, Key Biscayne presents a choice of good beaches. The broad, 5-mile (8km) stretch of public beach at Crandon Park is understandably popular, but the **Bill Baggs Cape Florida State Recreation Area** has much more to offer for a day out. The 500-acre (202ha) park has bicycling and walking trails, boardwalks and barbecues. Fishing is another popular pastime, and the 1845 Cape Florida lighthouse is open to the public.

➕ 17R

Bill Baggs Cape Florida State Recreation Area

✉ 1200 S. Crandon Boulevard ☎ 305/361-5811;

www.floridastateparks.org/capeflorida 🕐 Daily 8am–dusk ✋ Inexpensive

🍴 Snack concessions ($)

MIAMI BEACH

Miami Beach's golden shores are divided up into a number
of sections each patronized by a different clientele. The southern
reaches around South Pointe Park are popular with surfers and
Cuban families. The SoBe (South Beach) section between 5th and
21st Streets is the most hip, with a gay focus around 12th Street.
North of 21st Street, the crowd is more family-oriented, though
nude bathing is legal in the northern section of Haulover Park.

✚ 17R ✉ Ocean Drive and cross-streets off Collins Avenue. Boardwalk from
21st Street to 46th Street 🚌 K, S, M, C

MIAMI METROZOO

This huge and attractively laid out zoo
is home to more than 800 animals
most of them housed in spacious
natural habitat enclosures. The
monorail is a good way to get an
overview of what is on offer; then be
sure to stop off at the Bengal tigers,

the koalas, the Himalayan black bears and pygmy hippos, and the gorillas. There are wildlife shows throughout the day, and Dr. Wilde's Wonders of Tropical America offers activities for children.
www.miamimetrozoo.com

➕ *Downtown Miami 3f (off map)* ✉ 12400 S.W. 152nd Street, South Miami ☎ 305/251-0400 🕐 Daily 9:30–5:30

MIAMI SEAQUARIUM

Performances by Lolita the killer whale, Flipper the dolphin and Salty the sea lion are among the highlights at this venerable sealife attraction. In between the shows and the popular Shark Channel presentations, there are dozens of aquarium displays to inspect, petting experiences and the gently educational manatee exhibit. The Seaquarium is a leading marine research center and operates a Marine Mammal Rescue Team which cares for injured manatees. These huge but gentle creatures that live in shallow waters are often the victims of boat propellers.
www.miamiseaquarium.com

➕ *Downtown Miami 3f (off map)* ✉ 4400 Rickenbacker Causeway, Virginia Key ☎ 305/361-5705 🕐 Daily 9:30–5 💲 Expensive 🍽 Concessions and cafés ($–$$) 🚌 B

MIAMI MUSEUM OF SCIENCE AND SPACE TRANSIT PLANETARIUM

A first-class science museum with a raft of imaginative interactive exhibits, this is the place to sample virtual reality basketball, climb a rock wall or enjoy the traveling Smithsonian Exhibitions program. The natural world is represented in the coral reef and Everglades displays and there is a Wildlife Center where rescued birds and reptiles are rehabilitated for release back into the wild. The Space Transit Planetarium holds regular astronomical presentations.

www.miamisci.org

✚ *Downtown Miami 3f (off map)* ✉ 3280 S. Miami Avenue, Coconut Grove ☎ 305/646-4200 🕓 Daily 10–6 ✋ Moderate 🍴 Café ($) 🚈 Metrorail Vizcaya 🚌 48

MONKEY JUNGLE

Monkey Jungle's special appeal is the free-roaming macaque monkey colony released by Joe DuMond in 1933. Instead of locking up the monkeys at his behavioral research facility turned sightseeing attraction, DuMond decided to cage the visitors by enclosing boardwalk trails through the woodlands. While the descendants of the original six monkeys now scamper about at liberty, most of the other inhabitants, from gibbons and colobus monkeys to tiny tamarins, are securely caged. Monkey programs and feeding times are scheduled throughout the day.

www.monkeyjungle.com

✚ 17R ✉ 14805 S.W. 216th Street, South Miami ☎ 305/235-1611 🕓 Daily 9:30–5 ✋ Expensive 🍴 Snack bar ($)

PARROT JUNGLE ISLAND

Over 3,000 exotic animals and 500 species of plants have an excellent jungle home on 18.6-acre (7.5ha) Watson Island between downtown Miami and South Beach. The parrots reside at a re-creation of the cliffs of Manu, a natural habitat in Peru, while the pink flamingos made famous in the credits to the popular 1980s

television series *Miami Vice* can also be found here. There's an Everglades habitat, where pride of place is taken by a rare albino alligator, and Jungle Theater plays host to regular animal shows.

www.parrotjungle.com

✚ 17R ✉ 1111 Parrot Jungle Trail, off 395, Miami Beach ☎ 305/400-7000

⊗ Daily 10–6 🐾 Expensive

🍴 Lakeside Café ($)

VIZCAYA MUSEUM AND GARDENS

Millionaire industrialist James Deering had this splendid Italian Renaissance-style villa constructed as a winter residence between 1914 and 1916. Together with his architect, F. Burrell Hoffman Jr., and designer, Paul Chalfin, Deering trawled Europe for the 15th- to

19th-century antiques that furnish the Renaissance dining room, the rococo salon and the English-style Adams Library. The formal gardens that lead down to Biscayne Bay are peopled by a wealth of statuary and enclosed by native hardwood trees, while the dock is styled after a Venetian water landing.

www.vizcayamuseum.org

✚ *Downtown Miami 3f (off map)* ✉ 3251 S. Miami Avenue, Coconut Grove
☎ 305/250-9133 🕐 Daily 9:30–5 ✋ Moderate 🍴 Vizcaya Café ($–$$)
🚇 Metrorail Vizcaya 🚌 48

HOTELS

♛♛ Beachcomber Hotel ($$)

This is a modest boutique hotel in the heart of SoBe. The art deco hotel has large rooms, air-conditioning, cable TV, minibar, WiFi, a bistro and a 24-hour concierge. The wide front porch is a perfect place to watch the action.

✉ 1340 Collins Avenue ☎ 305/531-3755; www.beachcombermiami.com

♛♛ ♛♛ Biltmore Hotel ($$$)

The luxurious 1920s Mediterranean Revival-style landmark has grand public rooms and spacious accommodations. There is an excellent restaurant; a magnificent outdoor swimming pool, tennis and golf.

✉ 1200 Anastasia Avenue, Coral Gables ☎ 305/445-1926 or 1-800 727 1926; www.biltmorehotel.com

♛♛♛ Cadet Hotel ($–$$)

A very plain, unassuming hotel a few blocks from the fabled Delano, the Cadet may not be fancy, but it does offer a charming porch café/garden and 38 crisp rooms done in the obligatory art deco style with bamboo floors and Egyptian linens.

✉ 1701 James Avenue ☎ 305/672-6688; www.cadethotel.com

♛♛ Days Inn Oceanside ($–$$)

As this hotel is slightly north of SoBe, you can expect to pay lower rates – but you're right on the ocean. Not a bad trade-off. Rooms have double or king-size beds, with a pool, breakfast café and bar and grill making this a one-stop shop.

✉ 4299 Collins Avenue ☎ 305/673-1513; www.daysinn.com

♛♛ ♛♛ Doral Golf Resort and Spa ($$–$$$)

This place will suit golfers and their families, with five championship courses – it's hosted the PGA Tour since 1962 – and a luxury spa. There's also a superb water park and program of children's activities.

✉ 4400 87th Avenue ☎ 305/592-2000 or 1-800 713 6725; www.doralresort.com

❈❈ ❈❈ Mandarin Oriental ($$)

This is one of the best hotels in the US, offering superlative luxury, superb amenities and the highest levels of service. Rooms are cool and sophisticated, and each has a marble bathroom and a spacious balcony overlooking Biscayne Bay. There's a three-story spa and a health and fitness center, a private beach and a range of organized activities. The restaurant has won many awards.

✉ 500 Brickell Key Drive ☎ 305/913-8288 or 1-866 888 6780; www.mandarinoriental.com/miami

❈❈ Miami River Inn ($$)

A lovely 40-room hotel in Little Havana with lots of character, including hardwood floors and antique-furnished rooms. There's an outdoor pool and spa tub.

✉ 118 SW South River Drive ☎ 305/305-0045 or 1-800 468 3589; www.miamiriverinn.com

❈❈❈ Wyndham Miami Beach Resort ($$$)

This huge, refurbished hotel is right on the oceanfront and offers excellent water sports facilities. It is particularly good for families with children.

✉ 4833 Collins Avenue, Miami Beach ☎ 305/532-3600 or 1-800 221 8844

RESTAURANTS

❈ 11th Street Diner ($)

This low-price retro diner serves classics such as meatloaf, burgers, shakes and "blue-plate" specials. Open 24 hours a day, it attracts night owls and budget-minded locals who don't need the attitude found at other eateries.

✉ 1065 Washington Avenue ☎ 305/534-6373 🕐 24 hours

❈❈ Balans ($–$$)

Terrific value for fashionable Lincoln Road Mall. Wide-ranging Mediterranean/Asian menu plus naughty-but-nice English desserts such as sticky toffee pudding. Outdoor seating offers an alternative to the ever-crowded interior.

✉ 1022 Lincoln Road, Miami Beach ☎ 305/534-9191 🕐 24 hours

♕♕ Bubba Gump Shrimp Company ($–$$)
A casual seafood eatery on mainland Miami is highlighted by, naturally, shrimp (fried, stuffed, New Orleans, with chips); bourbon mahi mahi; and "boat trash" – a combination platter of fried shrimp, slipper lobster and mahi mahi dusted with cajun spices.

✉ 401 Biscayne Boulevard (Bayside Marketplace) ☎ 305/379-8866
🕐 Lunch and dinner

♕♕♕ Café Prima Pasta ($$)
Be prepared to wait for a table at this excellent pasta place. Classic dishes are made with the freshest home-made pastas and sauces.

✉ 414 71st Street, North Miami Beach ☎ 305/867-0106 🕐 Lunch and dinner

♕♕ Café Tu Tu Tango ($$)
World food, from designer pizzas and Tex-Mex standards to Mediterranean salads and kebabs, dished up in a funky artist's loft setting.

✉ CocoWalk, 3015 Grand Avenue, Coconut Grove ☎ 305/529-2222
🕐 Lunch, dinner until late

♕♕♕ China Grill ($$$)
Not Chinese cuisine but one of the best "world cuisine" restaurants in Miami. It's popular with the in-crowd, so who you are sitting next to is as important as the food.

✉ 404 Washington Avenue, South Beach ☎ 305/534-2211 🕐 Lunch and dinner

♕♕ Joe's Stone Crab ($$)
Opened in 1913 and the most renowned stone crab eatery in the city, Joe's is an unassuming place amid the famed SoBe nightlife.

✉ 11 Washington Avenue, Miami Beach ☎ 1-800 780 2722 🕐 Lunch Tue–Sat, dinner daily

♕ Lincoln Road Café ($–$$)
Amidst the trendy restaurants of SoBe is this sidewalk café that serves filling breakfasts as well as hearty lunches and dinners that

include seafood stew, beef medallions in mushroom sauce, chicken cordon bleu and lamb shanks.

✉ 943 Lincoln Rd ☎ 305/538-8066 🕔 Breakfast, lunch and dinner

❦❦ News Café ($)

See page 59.

❦❦❦ Nobu Miami Beach ($$$)

One of the "must visit" restaurants in SoBe, with a raft of celebrity clients. The sushi is excellent and interior is ultra chic.

✉ 1901 Collins Avenue (at the Shore Club) ☎ 305/695-3100 🕔 Dinner daily

❦❦❦❦ Norman's ($$$)

Chef Norman Van Aken is considered one of the founders of "world cuisine," the fusion of North American, Latin, Caribbean and Asian styles of cooking. Fresh ingredients and a wood-burning stove contribute to the exceptional flavors.

✉ 21 Almeria Avenue, Coral Gables ☎ 305/446-6767 🕔 Dinner daily

❦ Picnics at Allen's Drug Store ($)

It's nostalgia city at this old-fashioned all-American diner, complete with a jukebox and ice-cream sodas. As befits such surroundings, the best bets are the home-cooked chilli, deli sandwiches, burgers and Key lime pie.

✉ 6500 Bird Road, South Miami ☎ 305/665-6964 🕔 Breakfast, lunch and dinner

❦❦❦ Restaurant St. Michel ($$$)

Excellent standards of service and an elegant dining room set the scene for the superb, French-influenced New American cuisine.

✉ 162 Alcazar Avenue, Coral Gables ☎ 305/446-6572 🕔 Breakfast, lunch and dinner

❦❦ Trattoria Da Leo ($$)

This popular Italian restaurant spills out onto the Lincoln Road Mall and makes a good lunch stop as well as an evening venue.

✉ 819 Lincoln Road, Miami Beach ☎ 305/674-0350 🕔 Lunch and dinner

✈✈ Van Dyke Café ($–$$)

One of the best places in Miami for food and service, this café on Lincoln Road places you right in the epicenter of the action. Exemplary service belies the casual atmosphere, and modest prices on sandwiches, salads, chicken, steak and fish dishes. A second-floor jazz bar adds to the appeal.

✉ 846 Lincoln Road ☎ 305/534-3600 🕐 Breakfast, lunch and dinner

✈ Versailles ($$)

A legend in its own lifetime, this Little Havana institution is a living slice of Latin American soap opera with food, serving up a massive menu of Cuban goodies to crowds of tourists and partying Cubanos dressed up to the nines. Lots of fun and open late.

✉ 3555 S.W. 8th Street, Little Havana ☎ 305/444-0240 🕐 Lunch and dinner

SHOPPING

Bal Harbour Shops

A luxurious collection of European designer boutiques and the top US department stores Neiman Marcus and Saks Fifth Avenue in Miami's most exclusive shopping mall.

✉ 9700 Collins Avenue, Miami Beach ☎ 305/866-0311

Bayside Marketplace

See page 76.

CocoWalk

Boutiques, bistros and souvenirs at the heart of the fun Coconut Grove shopping district. More of the same at the streets of Mayfair, 2911 Grand Avenue.

✉ 3015 Grand Avenue, Coconut Grove ☎ 305/444-0777

Lincoln Road Mall

See page 70.

ENTERTAINMENT

Café Nostalgia
A taste of pre-Revolutionary hedonism, live Cuban music and lashings of nostalgia in Little Havana.
✉ 2212 SW 8th Street ☎ 305/541-2631 ⏰ Thu–Sun 9pm–3am

Clevelander
A bar and Ocean Drive landmark with exceptional people-watching potential.
✉ 1020 Ocean Drive, Miami Beach ☎ 305/531-3485 ⏰ Nightly until 5am

Club Deep
Has a 2,000-gallon aquarium underneath the dance floor. Dance and Latin music.
✉ 621 Washington Avenue ☎ 305/532-1509 ⏰ Nightly 10–5

Club Tropigala
Big-production, heavily besequinned musical revues to delight those who appreciate the full-on Las Vegas showtime approach.
✉ Fontainebleau Hilton, 4441 Collins Avenue, Miami Beach ☎ 305/672-7469 ⏰ Nightly

The Improv
Miami's comedy showcase for the established and not-so-established.
✉ 3390 Mary Street ☎ 305/441-8200 ⏰ Tue–Sun

Jazid
This cool jazz venue in SoBe is just the place to simmer away on a tropical evening.
✉ 1342 Washington Avenue, Miami Beach ☎ 305/673-9372 ⏰ Nightly

Opium
Three different areas to enjoy the latest dance tunes. Currently a hot spot for the "in crowd."
✉ 136 Collins Avenue ☎ 305/531-5535 ⏰ Tue and Thu–Sun 10–5

Tobacco Road

Historic live blues venue in the heart of the downtown district, which also hosts regular jazz nights.

✉ 626 S Miami Avenue ☎ 305/374-1198 🕒 Nightly until 5am

Van Dyke Café

Upstairs at the Van Dyke offers a great café-restaurant setting (► 91) for some of the best jazz acts around plus blues and Latin American sounds..

✉ 846 Linclon Road, Miami Beach ☎ 305/534 3600 🕒 Nightly

SPORT

Biscayne National Park Tours

It's all here: Azure blue waters, emerald islands, and sparkling coral reefs. Guided and self-guided tours by boat or on foot, with camping, snorkeling, diving, boating, fishing, picnicking and wildlife viewing.

✉ Convoy Point, 9700 S.W. 328th Street, Homestead ☎ 305/230-1100

Florida Marlins

The two-time World Series champions have proven they're one of the best teams in the major leagues, but with Miami's beaches and assorted diversions, fans haven't expressed much passion.

✉ Pro Player Stadium, 2267 Dan Marino Boulevard ☎ 305/626-7328

Homestead-Miami Speedway

Watch professionals compete in a series of high-octane races including NASCAR, Indy Racing League, and the Craftsman Truck Series.

✉ 1 Speedway Boulevard ☎ 305/230-7223 or 1-866 409 7223

Miami Dolphins

Although they haven't played in a Super Bowl game since 1984, this is the only team to play an undefeated season (17–0 in 1972) and they remain a Florida favorite.

✉ Pro Player Stadium, 2269 Dan Marino Boulevard, Miami Beach
☎ 305/643-7100 or 1-800 462 2637

Miami Heat

Credit superstar Shaquille O'Neal for helping make the Heat one of the state's most popular teams – as well as the 2006 National Basketball Association champions. They play in the new American Airlines Arena.

✉ Miami Arena, 701 Arena Boulevard, Miami Beach ☎ 305/530-4400

Palm Beach Polo, Golf and Country Club

One of the largest polo clubs in the world, there are several natural grass polo fields, with two that are part of stadiums. The main stadium seats approximately 5,000, so grab a seat and maybe you'll see Prince Charles get a good chukker going.

✉ 11199 Polo Club Road, Wellington, Miami Beach ☎ 561/798-7000

Sony-Ericsson Open

Held each spring (March–April) at the Tennis Center at Crandon Park, it's considered one of the most prestigious tournaments on the Association of Tennis Professionals (ATP) and Women's Tennis Association (WTA) tours.

✉ Tennis Center at Crandon Park, Key Biscayne, Miami Beach ☎ 305/442-3367; www.sonyericssonopen.com

South Beach Divers

Dive instruction as well as one-day dive and snorkel trips to Key Largo's John Pennekamp Marine Sanctuary.

✉ 850 Washington Avenue, Miami Beach ☎ 305/531-6110

South Florida and the Keys

**Less than a century ago,
southern Florida was pioneer
territory dominated by the
mysterious, waterlogged
expanses of the Everglades. It is
hard to believe today, for this is
Florida's most populous
and most visited
tourist heartland.**

Bordering the beleaguered Everglades,
the Gold Coast unfurls seamlessly north from Miami to West Palm
Beach, combining the accessible attractions of Fort Lauderdale
with more exclusive haunts such as Boca Raton and Palm Beach.
The southern Gulf coast is only slightly less developed between
the twin poles of upscale Naples and Fort Myers. The latter, with a
wide range of sightseeing possibilities and the lovely barrier
islands of Sanibel and Captiva (➤ 50–51), makes an especially
good destination for a family vacation.

Trailing off toward the tropics, the Florida Keys provide a
somewhat different brand of hospitality and a relaxed style that
captures the hearts of many visitors.

BISCAYNE NATIONAL PARK

A 181,500-acre (62,600ha) park with a surprising difference: more than 96 percent of this preserve is under water. It protects a live coral reef, which is home to more than 200 varieties of tropical fish, and an 18-mile (29km) chain of unspoiled island keys notable for marine and bird life. Snorkel and dive trips can be arranged from the Visitor Center at Convoy Point and glass-bottom boat tours offer an alternative window on the underwater world.
www.nps.gov/bisc

 17R 9700 SW 328th Street, Homestead ☎ 305/230-1100 ✪ Daily 8–5:30. Visitor Center: daily 8:30–5
🖐 Inexpensive

BOCA RATON

The well-heeled Gold Coast city of Boca Raton is a vision of strawberry ice-cream pink mansions and malls inspired by its 1920s founder Addison Mizner, who planned to make it the "greatest resort in the world." The land boom crash of 1926 ended his grandiose scheme, but several Mizner creations survive, including the exclusive Boca Raton Resort and Club.

Boca has the aura of a giant country

club offering golf, tennis, water sports and some superb beach parks. The two most exclusive (and pink) shopping malls are the Royal Palm Plaza and Mizner Park, with their classy little boutiques and galleries. Art lovers also have a treat in store at the **Boca Raton Museum of Art,** which stages frequently changing exhibitions and is home to the Mayers Collection of works by such artists as Degas, Picasso and Matisse, as well as a sculpture garden.

www.ci.boca-raton.fl.us/

🞧 18P 🔢 Boca Festival Days, Aug

Boca Raton Museum of Art

🖂 501 Plaza Real ☎ 561/392-2500 🕓 Tue, Thu, Fri 10–5, Wed 10–9, Sat–Sun 12–5 🖐 Inexpensive

CAPTIVA ISLAND

Best places to see, ➤ 50–51.

CORKSCREW SWAMP SANCTUARY

The National Audubon Society first posted guards on Corkscrew Swamp in 1912 to protect herons and egrets from plume hunters. The 11,000-acre (4,450ha) sanctuary is now renowned for its superb bird life and the nation's largest stand of giant bald cypress trees. An excellent 2.25-mile (4km) boardwalk trail traverses the shadowy swamp woodlands, where ancient cypress trees tower up to 130ft (40m) high. Some of these rare survivors of the 1940s and 50s Everglades logging booms are over 500 years old. Look for wading birds feeding and there may be a glimpse of an alligator or otters.

www.corkscrew.audubon.org

✚ 15P ✉ 375 Sanctuary Road, West Naples, (exit 111 on I75) ☎ 239/348-9151 🕓 Apr 12–Sep daily 7–7:30; Oct–Apr 11 7–5:30. Park gates close 1 hour before official closing 👪 Moderate

EVERGLADES NATIONAL PARK

The base of the Florida peninsula is like a giant sieve slowly draining the Everglades into the Gulf of Mexico through the maze of the Ten Thousand Islands. The "river of grass" begins its journey to the sea at Lake Okeechobee and flows southwest into the 1.5 million-acre (600,000ha) national park, which is a mere fifth of the Everglades' actual size.

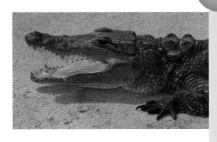

The park has three entrances, with the main visitor center on the eastern side. From here, a variety of short boardwalk trails venture into the sea of sawgrass dotted with island hammocks, which offer the best chance of spotting the flora and fauna; ranger-led walks and boat rentals are also available from some of the visitor centers. Tram tours depart from the northern Shark Valley entrance on US41, 35 miles (56km) west of Miami.

Canoe rentals and tours are available from the western Gulf Coast Visitor Center, near Everglades City.

www.nps.gov/ever/

🚩 16R ✉ Main Visitor Center, SR9336 (west of US1) ☎ 305/242-7700 🕐 Daily 8–5 ✋ Inexpensive (tickets valid for 7 days) 🍴 Flamingo ($–$$)

Gulf Coast Visitor Center

✉ CR29, Everglades City ☎ 239/695-3311 🕐 Daily 7:30–5 in winter, reduced in summer

The Gold Coast

A leisurely day-trip with time for sightseeing, this drive follows the Gold Coast north between Fort Lauderdale and Palm Beach.

Begin at the intersection of Sunrise Boulevard and South Ocean Boulevard (A1A), and head north on A1A for 14 miles (23km) to the intersection with Camino Real in Boca Raton. Turn left, passing the Boca Raton Resort and Country Club, then turn right on Federal Highway. Cross Palmetto Park Road and turn right to Mizner Park.

Window-shopping at Mizner Park is a favorite pastime in ostentatious Boca Raton (▶ 96–97).

Return to Palmetto Park Road. For the direct route to Palm Beach, turn left and rejoin A1A. For an interesting detour, turn right. At Powerline Road (4.5 miles/7km), turn right and head north for 5.75 miles (9km) to the Morikami Museum and Japanese Gardens.

Set in peaceful formal gardens, Japanese cultural exhibits and artifacts are displayed in the Yamoto-kan villa and museum.

Turn left out of the Morikami. At the intersection with Atlantic Avenue/SR806, turn right and continue through Deerfield Beach. Rejoin A1A north for 15 miles (24km) to a junction

*outside Palm Beach.
Bear right for A1A
north on South
Ocean Boulevard.
Just under a mile
(1.6km) later, keep
right on Ocean
Boulevard for just
over a mile (1.6km),
then turn left on to
Worth Avenue.*

Worth Avenue is the
gold-plated heart of
downtown Palm Beach
(➤ 44–45).

*For a fast return to
Fort Lauderdale, take
Royal Palm Way (five
blocks north of
Worth) across to
West Palm Beach and
follow signs for I-95.*

Distance 50 miles
(80.5km)
Time 2 hours or a day-trip
with stops
Start point Fort Lauderdale
✚ 17Q
End point Palm Beach
✚ 18P
Lunch Mark's at the Park
($) ✉ Mizner Park, Boca
Raton ☎ 561/395-0770

FORT LAUDERDALE

The largest city on the Gold Coast, Fort Lauderdale combines with ease its dual roles of thriving business and cultural center and popular beach resort. The namesake fort was founded on the New River in 1838, during the Second Seminole War, and the small settlement developed into a busy trading post before the arrival of the railroad. A special feature of the downtown district is the "Venice of America," a network of canals and islands dredged in the 1920s, which boasts some of the city's most desirable waterfront properties; these are best viewed from one of the regular sightseeing cruises.

The New River meanders through the city center conveniently linking a handful of historic sites and modern cultural landmarks with the 1.5-mile (2.5km) Riverwalk. This landscaped route along the north bank begins at the early 19th-century **Stranahan House,** the oldest surviving house in town. The pioneering Stranahans used to entertain railroad baron Henry Flagler in their heart pine parlor, and the interior faithfully recreates a Florida home of 1913–15. There is a small local history museum in a former inn in the Old Fort Lauderdale

district, and the Riverwalk ends at the Broward Center for Performing Arts.

Fort Lauderdale's main shopping and dining district is Las Olas Boulevard, an energetic, attractive, tree-shaded commercial boulevard that leads to the **Museum of Art.** The striking museum building is a fitting showcase for extensive collections of 19th- and 20th-century European and American art and visiting exhibitions. Nearby, the **Museum of Discovery and Science** is one of Florida's finest, with a spectacular range of exhibits, interactive displays and an IMAX cinema.

Hidden by hardwood hammock behind Fort Lauderdale's sandy beach, the **Bonnet House** is a delightful Old Florida relic. The 1920 plantation-style house was built by artist Frederic Bartlett and the interior is an eccentric work of art covered in murals, canvases and decorations fashioned out of beachcombing treasures. In the gardens, black and

white Australian swans paddle about a miniature lake flanked by the yellow bonnet lilies after which the house is named.

South along the oceanfront, the "Yachting Capital of the World" has its HQ at the Bahia Mar marina, where the *Jungle Queen* riverboat departs for New River cruises. Ocean-going voyages set out from Port Everglades, the world's second largest cruise-ship terminal.

✚ 17Q ❓ Fort Lauderdale Boat Show, Oct

Stranahan House

✉ 335 E. Las Olas Boulevard (at S.E. 6th Avenue) ☎ 954/524-4736
🕐 Wed–Sat 10–3, Sun 1–3 ✋ Inexpensive

Museum of Art

✉ 1 E. Las Olas Boulevard
☎ 954/525-5500 🕐 Daily 11–9
✋ Moderate

Museum of Discovery and Science

✉ 401 S. W. 2nd Street
☎ 954/467-6637; www.mods.org
🕐 Mon–Sat 10–5, Sun 12–6
✋ Moderate 🍴 Subway Café ($)

Bonnet House

✉ 900 N Birch Road ☎ 954/563-5393; www.bonnethouse.org
🕐 Tue–Sat 10–4, Sun 12–4. Last tour 2:30 ✋ Moderate

FORT MYERS

Inventor Thomas Alva Edison put Fort Myers on the map back in the 1880s, when he built himself a winter home in town and planted the first stretch of palms along McGregor Boulevard. Fort Myers now likes to call itself the "City of Palms" and makes a relaxed family vacation resort.

The **Edison Winter Home** and the **Ford Winter Home** next door, built by Edison's motoring magnate friend Henry Ford, are the most visited sights on the local tourist trail. Visits to the Edison home include a tour of the laboratory, which is packed with examples of the great man's inventions, from the phonograph to miner's lamps. Take time to explore the gardens too, which are planted with rare and exotic plants that were collected by Edison.

Junior scientists will have a field day at the colorful and entertaining **Imaginarium Hands-On Museum and Aquarium** with its impressive store of interactive games and gadgets, saltwater and freshwater aquariums, and a movie theater presenting 3-D film shows. At the **Calusa Nature Center and Planetarium** getting to grips with Florida's native flora and fauna is the name of the game. In addition to snake and alligator

presentations, there are bugs, lizards and touch exhibits, plus nature trails and the Audubon Aviary, a rescue and rehabilitation unit for injured birds.

A short drive east of town, **Manatee World** is a non-captive haven for manatees. In winter, daily boat tours afford a prime view of the animals basking in the warm waters, and there are exhibits year round.

For animal-spotting with a bit more bite, make tracks for **Babcock Wilderness Adventures** and a bumpy swamp buggy ride around the vast Crescent B Ranch – the tour guides are trained naturalists. As well as bison, quarter horses and Senepol cattle, the ranch is home to wild alligators, hogs, deer and turkeys. The buggies also venture into 10,000-acre (4,000ha) Telegraph Swamp, where a boardwalk trail leads to a panther enclosure.

www.cityftmyers.com

🔒 15P

Edison Winter Home and Ford Winter Home

✉ 2350 McGregor Boulevard ☎ 239/334-3614 ⏰ Mon–Sat 9–4, Sun 12–4
✋ Moderate

Imaginarium Hands-On Museum and Aquarium

✉ 2000 Cranford Avenue ☎ 239/337-3332 ⏰ Mon–Sat 10–5, Sun 12–5
✋ Moderate 🍴 Imagateria Café ($)

Calusa Nature Center and Planetarium

✉ 3450 Ortiz Avenue ☎ 239/275-3435 ⏰ Mon–Sat 9–5, Sun 11–5
✋ Inexpensive

Manatee World

✉ 5605 Palm Beach Boulevard, SR80 (1.5 miles/2.5km east of I-75/Exit 25)
☎ 239/694-4042 ⏰ Summer daily 8–8, winter daily 8–5 ✋ Moderate

Babcock Wilderness Adventures

✉ 800 SR31 (9.5 miles/15km north of SR78), Punto Gorda
☎ 1-800 500 5583 ⏰ Nov–May daily 9–3; Jun–Oct mornings only
✋ Expensive ❓ Reservations essential

ISLAMORADA

The self-styled "Sport Fishing Capital of the World," Islamorada consists of a clutch of small islands with a concentration of marinas and Florida's second oldest marine park. Charter boats offer half- and full-day expeditions to the rich Gulf Stream fishing grounds. Local dive operators also do good business and there are trips to the uninhabited island preserves of Indian and Lignumvitae keys from Lower Matecumbe Key.

Sea lion and dolphin shows are on the bill at the **Theater of the Sea.** This old-style attraction includes all the usual shark encounters and touch tanks, and has added a Dolphin Adventure program which allows visitors to swim with captive dolphins. Understandably popular, the dolphin swim requires reservations.

✚ 17S ❓ Sport fishing tournaments throughout the year. For information ☎ 305/664-4503

Theater of the Sea

✉ 84721 Overseas Highway, Mile Marker 84.5 ☎ 305/664-2431 🕐 Daily 9:30–4 ✋ Expensive

KEY LARGO

Key Largo ("long island" to the early Spanish explorers) is the largest of the Florida Keys, and a lively resort within easy striking distance of Miami. The island makes a great base for divers, who can explore the depths of the magnificent **John Pennekamp Coral Reef State Park,** which extends for over 3 miles (5km) out to sea across the living coral reef. Snorkeling and dive trips, equipment and canoe rental, and a dive school are all available, and there are a range of glass-bottomed boat trips, aquariums in the visitor center and walking trails on the land-based portion of the park.

Local bird life is showcased at the **Florida Keys Wild Bird Center** on the neighboring island of Tavernier. This rescue and rehabilitation facility has a boardwalk trail past enclosures for hawks, ospreys, cormorants and pelicans. There are also birdwatching hides overlooking a salt pond where herons and roseate spoonbills come to feed.

🛧 17S ❓ Island Jubilee, Nov

John Pennekamp Coral Reef State Park

✉ Mile Marker 102.5 ☎ 305/451-1202 ⏱ Daily 8–5 ✋ Inexpensive

Florida Keys Wild Bird Center

✉ Mile Marker 93.6 ☎ 305/852-4486 ⏱ Daily dawn–dusk ✋ Donation

KEY WEST

Best places to see, ➤ 40–41.

LOWER KEYS

South of the minor miracle of the Seven Mile Bridge (in reality 110yds/99m short of 7 miles/11.2km), the Lower Keys are less developed than their northern counterparts. Just across the bridge, **Bahia Honda State Park** is one of the finest natural beaches in the Keys and a regular contender in any list of the nation's top ten beaches. Watersports concessions rent out equipment and snorkels, and behind the shore there are walking trails through tropical forest, where several rare trees and plants can be seen.

The other top attraction in this area is the **National Key Deer Refuge,** centered on Big Pine Key. The deer here are pint-sized relatives of the Virginia white-tailed deer and are best spotted in the early morning and evening. Key Deer Boulevard (Mile Marker 30.5) leads to Blue Hole, a freshwater lagoon in an old limestone quarry. Wading birds gather here to feed, and alligators and turtles occasionally put in an appearance. A little farther down the road, Watson's Nature Trail leads off into the forested heart of the refuge.

✚ 15T

Bahia Honda State Park
✉ Mile Marker 37 ☎ 305/872-2353
🕐 Daily 8–dusk 💷 Inexpensive

National Key Deer Refuge
✉ Refuge Visitor Center, 175 Key Deer Boulevard, Mile Marker 30.3 ☎ 305/872-2239 🕐 Refuge: open site. Headquarters: Mon–Fri 8–5 💷 Free

MARATHON

Strung out in a jumble of malls, motels and small businesses along US1 north of the Seven Mile Bridge, Marathon is the chief town of the Middle Keys, and a rival for Islamorada's sport fishing crown (➤ 107).

Another good reason to visit Marathon is the Museum of Natural History of the Florida Keys. Also, the Old Seven Mile Bridge (which doubles as the World's Longest Fishing Pier) gives access to **Pigeon Key,** a former construction workers' camp from the Flagler era restored as a National Historic District.

✚ 16T

Pigeon Key

✉ Visitor Center at Mile Marker 47 ☎ 305/743-5999 🕐 Daily 10–4
👐 Moderate

NAPLES

A relaxing, small resort city on the Gulf of Mexico, Naples has beautiful beaches, an attractively restored historic shopping and restaurant district in Third Street South, a thriving Center for the Arts and more than 50 championship golf courses.

Naples lies close enough to the Everglades to make a day-trip to the national park's western entrance near Everglades City (▶ 98–99). Closer to home, visitors to the Naples Nature Center can take to the water on a narrated boat ride, sample woodland nature trails and drop in at the Wildlife Rehabilitation Center, which tends over 1,600 native bird and animal casualties a year.

There are even more exotic beasts in store at **Caribbean Gardens,** a popular zoological park with a special interest in big cats. Daily shows put a selection of lions, tigers, leopards and cougars through their paces. Many of the animals are the result of the park's successful captive breeding programs.

✚ 15Q

Caribbean Gardens

✉ 1590 Goodlette-Frank Road ☎ 239/262-5409 🕔 Daily 9:30–5:30
✋ Expensive

PALM BEACH

Best places to see, ➤ 44–45.

SANIBEL ISLAND

Best places to see, ➤ 50–51.

WEST PALM BEACH

The high-rise downtown heart of West Palm Beach faces monied and manicured Palm Beach across the Intracoastal Waterway. While the super-rich cavort in the oceanfront resort, West Palm Beach takes care of business and provides a selection of shopping, cultural attractions and sightseeing opportunities.

The city's pride and joy is the **Norton Museum of Art,** one of the most important art museums in the southeastern US. Built around the collections of steel magnate Ralph Norton (1875–1953), the museum is particularly strong on French Impressionist and Post-Impressionist works (Monet, Matisse, Renoir, Gauguin, Chagall) and 20th-century American art (Hopper, O'Keeffe, Pollock), and has stunning Chinese ceramics, bronzes and jade carvings.

There are several good outings for children. For "hands-on" interactive fun, the South Florida Science Museum is a big hit.

Sparky electricity displays, booming sound waves and a mini tornado are among the treats on offer. Hands-off is the best way to approach the **Lion Country Safari,** a two-part wildlife park that provides some very close encounters with lions, elephants, rhinos and giraffes in the 500-acre (200ha) drive-through African safari section. In the Safari World Park next door there are more animals, fairground rides, lagoon cruises and a nature trail.

✚ 18P ❓ SunFest, Apr–May; Japanese Bon Festival, Aug

Norton Museum of Art

✉ 1451 S. Olive Avenue ☎ 561/832-5196; www.norton.org 🕓 Tue–Sat 10–5, Sun 1–5 (also Mon Nov–Apr) 🖑 Inexpensive

Lion Country Safari

✉ W. Southern Boulevard/ SR80 (17 miles/27km west of I-95) ☎ 561/793-1084; www.lioncountrysafari.com 🕓 Daily 9:30–5:30 🖑 Expensive

HOTELS

ISLAMORADA
♛♛♛ Cheeca Lodge ($$$)
Quiet, low-rise resort complex on the oceanside. Excellent fishing and diving, children's programs and fine dining.
✉ Mile Marker 82.5 ☎ 305/ 664-4651 or 1-800 327 2888

♛♛ Sands of Islamorada ($$–$$$)
An attractive waterfront resort with a pier for boating, fishing and snorkeling, a swimming pool and a hot tub under the palm trees.
✉ 80051 Overseas Highway ☎ 305/664-2791 or 888/741-4518

KEY LARGO
♛♛ Marina Del Mar Resort and Marina ($–$$$)
See page 64.

♛♛ Rock Reef Resort ($–$$)
Family-owned waterfront resort with verdant gardens, palm-shaded hammocks and private sandy beach. Rooms, apartments and cottages are available.
✉ 97850 Overseas Highwy ☎ 305/852-2401 or 1-800 477 2343

KEY WEST
♛♛♛ Cypress House ($$–$$$)
Set in an 1888 traditional "Conch" house, this grand bed-and-breakfast is only one block from the excitement of Duval Street. There's a swimming pool and rooms have air conditioning. Excellent Continental breakfast and cocktail hour included in the price.
✉ 601 Caroline Street ☎ 305/294-6969

Merlin Guest House ($$–$$$)
A tropical motif flows throughout the grounds and into 20 queen rooms, king suites and cottages. A Continental breakfast is served under the courtyard arbor, and the private, secluded pool is a great place to take a break.
✚ 811 Simonton Street ✉ 305/296-3336; merlinguesthouse.com

NAPLES
◥◥◥◥◥ Ritz Carlton Naples ($$$)

The height of luxury, set on the fabulous Naples beach, with its own spa, golf, tennis and water sports facility, plus the usual pools and fitness center. The resort has seven restaurants. Rooms are plush.

✉ 280 Vanderbilt Beach Road ☎ 239/598-3300

PALM BEACH
◥◥◥◥◥ The Breakers ($$$)

See page 64.

CAPTIVA ISLAND
◥◥◥ South Seas Island Resort ($$$)

See page 64.

RESTAURANTS

BOCA RATON
◥◥ Boca West Ale House ($$)

A warm ,welcoming hometown feel in a chain restaurant specializing in wings, hamburgers, chicken, seafood, steak – and more than 75 types of home-brewed beers and ales.

✉ 9244 W Glades Road ☎ 561/487-2989 🕐 Lunch and dinner

◥◥◥◥ Mark's at the Park ($$–$$$)

See page 58.

CAPTIVA ISLAND
◥◥ The Bubble Room ($$–$$$)

See page 58.

FORT LAUDERDALE
◥◥◥ Black Orchid Café ($$$)

Set beside the Intercoastal waterway, the Black Orchid offers a good range of dishes from chicken and seafood to unusual meats such as ostrich, buffalo and game.

✉ 2985 North Ocean Boulevard ☎ 954/561-9398 🕐 Dinner

♦♦ Shooters Waterfront Cafe

Festive dockside dining with a pool, patio and live entertainment.
Dine on rotisserie chicken, babyback ribs, and mango barbeque
swordfish while enjoying a panoramic waterfront view.

✉ 3033 N.E. 32nd Avenue ☎ 954/566-2855 🕐 Lunch and dinner

FORT MYERS

♦♦♦ The Veranda ($$)

Housed in a pretty early 19th-century historic home, the Veranda
also offers courtyard dining in the summer months. The excellent
menu regional menu uses fresh local produce.

✉ 2122 2nd Street ☎ 239/332-2065 🕐 Lunch (except Sat), dinner.
Closed Sun

ISLAMORADA

♦ Islamorada Fish Company ($$–$$$)

Started as a marina snack bar in the 1940s, this sprawling
waterfront restaurant has 150 seats on the water, and shrimp
skewers, yellowfin tuna, stone crab, mahi mahi, grouper, raw
oysters, sushi, and homemade soups on the menu.

✉ 81532 Overseas Highway ☎ 305/664-9271 🕐 Lunch and dinner

♦♦ Uncle's ($$)

The extensive menu focuses on fresh seafood, but there are lots
of chicken, veal, pasta, salads, vegetarian and low-fat options.

✉ 8090 Overseas Highway at Mile Marker 80.9 ☎ 305/664-4402 🕐 Dinner

KEY LARGO

♦♦ The Fish House Restaurant & Seafood Market ($$$)

A laid-back, none-too-fancy setting is part of the appeal of this
upper Keys restaurant near John Pennekamp Coral Reef Park.
Fresh local seafood (some caught just a few miles away) includes
yellowtail snapper, mahi-mahi, grouper, Florida lobster, smoked
fish and Conch-style cooking.

✉ 102401 Overseas Highway ☎ 305/451-4665 🕐 Lunch and dinner

KEY WEST

▼▼▼ Antonia's ($$$)

This restaurant is a long-established feature of Key West's eating out scene. Traditional recipes are prepared by chef Phillip Smith.

✉ 615 Duval Street ☎ 305/294-6565; www.antoniaskeywest.com

🕒 Mon–Fri lunch, dinner, Sat–Sun dinner only

▼▼ Blue Heaven ($$–$$$)

The motto is "No shoes, no shirt, no problem" at this laid-back spot with trestle tables in the yard and a bathtub full of chilled beer on the bar. Enjoy generous helpings of Caribbean barbecue shrimp, chicken jerk, and fresh snapper.

✉ 729 Thomas Street ☎ 305/296-8666 🕒 Lunch and dinner

▼▼ Jimmy Buffett's Margaritaville Cafe ($$–$$$)

Inspired by his 1977 hit, Buffett's Key West restaurant is hallowed ground for his fans. Live music, island drinks, seafood and chicken platters, and a party atmosphere in the real Margaritaville.

✉ 500 Duval Street ☎ 305/292-1435 🕒 Lunch and dinner

▼ Pepe's ($)

Sit at outdoor tables in a tree-shaded garden at this friendly local café diner to enjoy hearty breakfasts, seafood, steaks, and barbecued dishes.

✉ 806 Caroline Street ☎ 305/294-7192 🕒 Breakfast, lunch and dinner

▼ Pisces ($$$)

Upscale seafood restaurant serving up succulent lobster and other fruits de mer in imaginative concoctions devised by chef Andrew Berman.

✉ 1007 Simonton Street ☎ 305/294-7100 🕒 Dinner

NAPLES

▼▼ Tommy Bahama's Tropical Cafe ($$$)

With its West Indian atmosphere, dining here is like dining in the Tropics. The island decor complements Caribbean-inspired dishes.

✉ 1220 3rd Street South ☎ 239/643-6889 🕒 Lunch and dinner

✿✿ Mel's Diner ($$–$$$)

Low-key and comfortable with comfort foods to match. Blue plate specials include country-fried steak, mashed potatoes, chicken pot pie, and pot roast. Burgers, breakfast and desserts round out the daily offerings.

✉ 3650 Tamiami Trail ☎ 239/643-9898 ⊙ Breakfast, lunch, and dinner

PALM BEACH
✿✿✿ Leopard Lounge and Supper Club ($$$)

Leopard skin spots feature in the theatrical interior of this elegant supper club. Enjoy a tempting continental menu, excellent service and nightly entertainment.

✉ The Chesterfield Hotel, 363 Coconut Row ☎ 561/659-5800 ⊙ Lunch and dinner

SANIBEL
✿ Lazy Flamingo II ($$)

A casual spot with a nautical theme, Lazy Flamingo has the biggest bar on the island. There is a good choice of seafood, including a raw bar, plus burgers, prime rib sandwiches and Caesar salad.

✉ 1036 Periwinkle Way, Sanibel ☎ 239/472-6939 ⊙ Lunch and dinner

SHOPPING

Duval and Simonton Streets, Key West

See page 70.

Las Olas Boulevard, Fort Lauderdale

See page 70.

Prime Outlets at Florida City

South of Miami, 45 factory outlet stores offering 25 to 75 percent off retail prices on Levis, Nike footwear, OshKosh B'Gosh and more. There is also a food court and children's playground.

✉ 250 E. Palm Drive (off US1 and Florida Turnpike), Florida City
☎ 305/248-4727

Sawgrass Mills

The world's largest discount outlet mall with 350 name-brand stores and outlets.

✉ W. Sunrise Boulevard at Flamingo Road, Sunrise, Fort Lauderdale
☎ 954/846-2300

Tanger Sanibel Factory Outlet Stores

Just east of the Sanibel Causeway, this mainland outlet mall offers bargain prices on clothing, footwear, and accessories.

✉ 20350 Summerlin Road, Fort Myers ☎ 239/454 1974

Third Street South and the Avenues, Naples

See page 70.

Worth Avenue, Palm Beach

See page 70.

ENTERTAINMENT

O'Hara's Pub

O'Hara's in Fort Lauderdale is one of the top live jazz venues in the southeast. Also Sunday lunchtime sessions.

✉ 722 E. Las Olas Boulevard, Fort Lauderdale ☎ 954/524-1764 🕔 Nightly

Respectable Street Café

Progressive nightclub in West Palm beach's downtown entertainment and dining district. Theme nights from techno and rave to retro.

✉ 518 Clematis Street, West Palm Beach ☎ 561/832-9999 🕔 Tue–Sat from 9pm

Rick's

This popular Key West nightspot has live music downstairs and dancing in the Upstairs Bar.

✉ 202 Duval Street, Key West ☎ 305/296-5513 🕔 Café until 11pm; bar 8pm–4am

SPORT

Everglades Rentals & Eco Adventures

Canoe and kayak rentals, and day or overnight guided adventures, as well as powerboat shuttle service and re-supply runs to campsites and beaches.

✉ 107 Camilla Street, Everglades City ☎ 239/695-3299

Pro Dive

Snorkeling and scuba dives at a variety of sites within two miles of shore, including 10 meter coral reefs, 18 meter drift dives, and shipwrecks in water between 10 to 40 meters.

✉ 515 Seabreeze Boulevard/ A1A, Fort Lauderdale ☎ 954/776-3483

Dolphin Research Center

Guided tours of a facility where sea lions and bottlenose dolphins are cared for. As well as demonstrations of behaviours and jumps, the (expensive) highlight is the chance to swim with a dolphin.

✉ Grassy Key ☎ 305/289-1121

John Pennekamp Coral Reef State Park Dive Shop

America's only underwater state park starts a foot offshore and continues 3 miles (4.8km) into the Florida Straits. Swim in the lagoon, or sign up for glass-bottom boat tour, snorkeling, or scuba dives atop the most colorful and active reefs in North America.

✉ Mile Marker 102.5, Key Largo ☎ 305/451-6322

Dolphins Plus

Swim with sea lions and dolphins, enroll in the "Trainer for a Day" program, or settle for the more affordable educational tours.

✉ 31 Corrine Place (near MM 100), Key Largo ☎ 305/451-1993

Tarpon Bay Explorers Inc.

A variety of excursions within the fabulous J.N. Ding Darling National Wildlife Refuge include tram tours, canoe tours and bicycle tours to put you up close with the state's wildlife.

✉ 900 Tarpon Road (off Sanibel-Captiva Road near J. N. "Ding" Darling Wildlife Refuge), Sanibel ☎ 239/472-8900

Central Florida

Central Florida's very first theme park was housed in an Orlando fruit-packing warehouse, which had been converted into a skating rink during the icy winter of 1894–95. Leisure attractions have become rather more sophisticated of late (and are rarely as cold), and since the arrival of Walt Disney World, Orlando has been the undisputed gateway to theme park heaven.

Though it is easy for theme park addicts not to venture further afield, visitors in need of a reality check will find that central Florida has much more to offer. Sporting opportunities and state preserves abound, and there are country towns and beach resorts an easy day-trip away.

An hour's drive east of Orlando, sea turtles nest on the beach in the shadow of the Kennedy Space Center, one of the state's top attractions. To the west, the cities of St. Petersburg and Tampa offer an irresistible combination of notable sightseeing attractions and superb beaches.

BLUE SPRING STATE PARK

This attractive wooded park on the banks of the St. Johns River is one of the best places to see wild manatees in central Florida. During the winter months (November–March), manatees leave the cool river and gather here to bask in the warm waters produced from the turquoise blue depths of the park's namesake artesian spring at a constant 72°F (22°C). The spring head is a popular swimming hole and dive site. There are also woodland trails, boat trips and kayaks for rent.

www.floridastateparks.org

✚ 16J ✉ 2100 W. French Avenue, Orange City ☎ 386/775-3663 🕓 Daily 8–dusk 🖐 Inexpensive

CYPRESS GARDENS ADVENTURE PARK

Originally opened in 1936, one of Florida's oldest natural attractions closed briefly in 2003, but re-opened as a botanical garden with an added adventure park. If you prefer a slow pace, walk among the 150 lakeside acres (61ha) and formal gardens that contain more than 8,000 varieties of plants gathered from 90 countries. It's beautiful and calming in an old-fashioned Florida way. A faster pace is found in the daredevil ski shows and the amusement park's roller coasters, bumper cars, water slides, and kiddie rides. All in all, a diverse degree of entertainment that should please everyone.

www.cypressgardens.com

✚ 15L ✉ SR540 W. Winter Haven ☎ 863/324-2111 or 1-800 282 2123 🕓 Daily 10–6, extended summer hours ✋ Expensive

FANTASY OF FLIGHT

This major aviation museum combines historic aircraft exhibits with state-of-the-art simulator rides. Scale models and authentic aircraft trace the history of flight from the Wright brothers and daredevil antics of 1920s circus barnstormers through fighter aircraft from World War II and beyond. Try the flight simualtors or reserve a flight in an open cockpit biplane (additional charge).

www.fantasyofflight.com

✚ 15L ✉ SR559, Polk City ☎ 863/984-3500 🕓 Daily 10–5, extended summer hours ✋ Moderate

FLORIDA'S SPACE COAST

The big draw here is the terrific Kennedy Space Center (▶ 38–39). Within clear sight of the launch pad, the Space Coast can also offer the unspoiled dunes of the Canaveral National Seashore and the marshland wilderness area protected by **Merritt Island National Wildlife Refuge.** To the south, the 20-mile (32km) strip of barrier island beach between Cocoa Beach and Melbourne has been developed as a family resort.

www.space-coast.com

✚ 17K

Merritt Island Refuge

✉ SR406 (4 miles/6.5km east of Titusville)

☎ 321/861-0667 🕓 Visitor Center: Mon–Fri 8–4:30, Sat–Sun 9–5. Closed Sun Feb–Oct

FORT PIERCE

Founded on the site of a Seminole War army outpost, Fort Pierce's main claims to fame are the barrier beaches of Hutchinson Island across the Indian River. A favorite spot for snorkeling is Bathtub Beach, and surfers congregate at Fort Pierce State Recreation Area or Pepper Beach. Down near Stuart Beach, the **Elliott Museum** makes an interesting stop. It is named after inventor Sterling Elliott and contains historic and eccentric exhibits.

➕ 17M

Elliott Museum

✉ 825 N.E. Ocean Boulevard/A1A ☎ 772/225-1961 🕐 Mon–Sat 10–4, Sun 1–4 ✋ Moderate

GAMBLE PLANTATION

The last remaining antebellum house in southern Florida, this gracious two-story mansion was built by sugar planter Major Robert Gamble in the 1840s. Two foot-thick (0.6m) walls and through breezes help keep the house cool in summer and the interior has been restored and furnished with period antiques. At the height of its productivity around 200 slaves worked Gamble's 3,500-acre (1,400ha) plantation and tours of the house include many interesting snippets of information about plantation life.

www.floridastateparks.org

➕ 14M ✉ 3708 Patten Avenue (US301 E.), Ellenton ☎ 941/723-4536 🕐 Daily 8–dusk. Visitor center: 8–4:30; tours Mon, Thu–Sun 9:30, 10:30, 1, 2, 3, 4 ✋ Inexpensive

HOMOSASSA SPRINGS
STATE WILDLIFE PARK

One of Florida's original
natural tourist attractions,
Homosassa Springs is a favorite manatee playground and
showcase for several of the state's other endangered animal
species. An underwater observatory in the 46ft-deep (14m)
spring gives an unusual perspective on life in the Homosassa
River, while pontoon boat rides are good for wildlife-spotting
along the riverbank. Look for alligators, otters and native birds.
Florida black bears, bob cats and deer can be seen in natural
habitat enclosures.

www.floridastateparks.org; **www.**manateecam.com

✚ 14J ✉ 4150 S. Suncoast Boulevard/US19, Homosassa ☎ 352/628-5343
⏰ Daily 9–5:30 👆 Moderate 🍴 Concessions ($)

JUNO BEACH MARINELIFE CENTER

Each summer between June and August, Juno Beach is transformed into a major loggerhead sea turtle nesting ground. The excellent Marinelife Center has turtle tanks and a turtle nursery, natural history and marine displays, and organizes guided beach walks (reservations advised).

www.marinelife.org

🔒 18N ✉ 14200 US1, Juno Beach ☎ 561/627-8280 🕐 Mon–Sat 10–5, Sun 10–4 ✋ Inexpensive

JUPITER

Once the northern terminus of the 1880s Lake Worth Railroad, which numbered Mars, Venus and Juno among its stops, Jupiter's landmark red lighthouse is hard to miss. It's an offshoot of the Burt Reynolds' Ranch, a strange exercise in hagiography filled with memorabilia. More interesting is the **Florida Lighthouse and Museum,** with collections of Native American and pioneer artifacts.

🔒 17N

Florida Lighthouse and Museum

✉ 805 N. US1 ☎ 561/747-6639 🕐 Tue–Sun 10–5
✋ Inexpensive

KENNEDY SPACE CENTER

Best places to see, ➤ 38–39.

KISSIMMEE

A budget dormitory annex for Walt Disney World to the south of Orlando, Kissimmee stretches for more than 20 miles (32km) along US192 in a seamless strip of hotels, motels, shopping malls and family restaurants. To help visitors find their way around,

Navigational Markers (NM) have been posted along the route.

Along the main road (US192), family-style attractions range from miniature golf and fairground rides outside the Old Town Kissimmee shopping mall (► 151) to dinner theaters. **A World of Orchids** (12 miles/19km west) has a half-acre (0.2ha) conservatory housing thousands of orchids and hundreds of tropical plants alongside chameleons and birds. If you'd prefer to study native Floridian flora and fauna, then take to the water on Boggy Creek Airboat Rides. The half-hour rides offer close-up encounters with alligators, water birds and turtles.

Just north of Kissimmee, the old-fashioned but enduringly popular **Gatorland** features hundreds of alligators, 'gator-wrestling shows, educational presentations, an assortment of turtles and snakes, and a boardwalk trail through a marshland alligator breeding ground and bird preserve.

www.kissimmee.org

✚ 15L

A World of Orchids

✉ 2501 N. Old Lake Wilson Road (CR545) ☎ 407/396-1887 🕔 Mon–Sat 9:30–4:30 ✋ Moderate

Gatorland

✉ 14501 S. Orange Blossom Trail/US441 ☎ 407/855-5496 or 1-800 393 5297; www.gatorland.com 🕔 Daily 9–dusk ✋ Expensive ✋ Moderate

MOUNT DORA

A pretty lakeside country town set in the citrus groves north of Orlando, Mount Dora was founded back in the 1870s. The restored downtown district offers an attractive selection of gift shops, galleries and cafés, there are boat trips and walks around the lake, and the Chamber of Commerce distributes drive tour maps to the town's historic Victorian homes.

www.mountdora.com

✚ 15K 🍴 Windsor Rose English Tea Room ($–$$), 144 W. 4th Avenue ☎ 352/383-2165 ❓ Drive tour maps from Chamber of Commerce, 341 Alexander Street

OCALA

The rolling pastures of Marion County are the center of Florida's billion-dollar horse-breeding industry, bordering the vast pinewood preserve of the Ocala National Forest. Ten miles (16km) east

of Ocala, the 400,000-acre (160,000ha) national forest offers a range of outdoor activities including excellent hiking trails, fishing, boating, swimming and some of the most attractive canoe trails in the state.

On the edge of the forest, glass-bottom boat rides at **Silver Springs** have been a local sightseeing feature since 1878. The world's largest artesian spring is now part of a theme park attraction with Silver River cruises, exotic animals and Jeep safaris touring the woodlands.

www.ocalacc.com

✚ 14J ❓ Details of horse farm visits: Ocala Chamber of Commerce, 110 E. Silver Springs Boulevard ☎ 352/629 8051

Silver Springs

✉ 5656 E. Silver Springs Boulevard ☎ 352/236-2121; www.silversprings.com ⏱ Daily 10–5 (extended summer and hols)

✋ Very expensive

ORLANDO

Launched into the limelight by the opening of Disney's Magic
Kingdom® in 1971, Orlando is the undisputed world capital of
theme parks and a bustling modern city 15 miles
(24km) north of the Walt Disney World® Resort
(► 142–145). The main tourist area is in the south
around International Drive, or I-Drive. It runs parallel
to the I-4 highway, which helps cut journey times
between the city's widely spread attractions.

The biggest attraction on (or just off) I-Drive is
Universal Orlando® Resort, with its two theme
parks, and the Universal CityWalk® shopping, dining
and entertainment district. Universal Studios®'s top
rides include Revenge of the Mummy – The Ride,
the interactive MEN IN BLACK™ Alien Attack™ and
the brand new Simpson's ride. Another don't miss is
the excellent Terminator 2®: 3-D show. At Islands of
Adventure®, other must-sees including the

Incredible Hulk Coaster®, Dueling Dragons® Roller Coaster and the do-not-miss Amazing Adventures of Spider-Man®.

The second theme park, Universal's Islands of Adventure®, is a homage to the comicstrip. Guests receive a ticket to ride the cartoons from the height of The Incredible Hulk Coaster® and Doctor Doom's Fearfall® to the depths of Popeye and Bluto's Bilge-Rat Barges® raft ride. Touted as the world's most technologically advanced theme park it is also the place to get to grips with the fantastic robotic models of Jurassic Park®, the fantasy world of The Lost Continent® and the whimsical Seuss Landing™.

Heading south of I-Drive, **SeaWorld** is Orlando's other major theme park. The world's most popular marine park offers a full day of entertaining shows starring killer whales, dolphins, sea lions and more. In between the shows, there are fantastic aquarium displays, the enchanting Penguin Encounter, manatees, touch tanks, polar bears and beluga whales as well as the Kraken roller coaster and Journey To Atlantis thrill ride. SeaWorld's sister park, **Discovery Cove,** specialises in interactive marine adventures. Park admission is restricted to 1,000 visitors a day and the lucky

few can experience a raft of water-based activities including snorkeling in the Coral Reef pool and swimming with bottlenose dolphins.

Downtown Orlando rises in a miniature forest of mirrored glass towers on the shores of Lake Eola. Wonderworks on I-Drive offers interactive games, concentrating on fun science exhibits. To skydive without a parachute, visit SkyVenture, which

places you atop a mammoth blow dryer to keep you floating in mid-air. The area has attracted numerous restaurants and bars.

To the north, the terrific **Orlando Science Center** is one of the best science museums in the state. Laid out on four levels the museum is packed with dozens of eye-catching and entertaining interactive exhibits and a planetarium.

Nearby, the gorgeous **Harry P. Leu Gardens** offer gentle strolls on the banks of Lake Rowena and impressive formal rose gardens. In springtime the magnolias burst into color, with a spectacular show of camellias planted by the Leus, who lived at the heart of the gardens. Their home is open for tours.

The pretty northeastern suburb of Winter Park also makes a delightful escape from the crowds. There is upscale shopping on Park Avenue, boat trips on Lake Osceola, and a superb collection of Tiffany glassware and art nouveau at the Morse Gallery of Art. **www.**orlandoinfo.com

✚ 16K 🚌 I-Ride service along International Drive between Belz Factory Mall and SeaWorld

Universal Orlando® Resort

✉ 1000 Universal Studios Plaza ☎ 407/363-8000 or 1-888 837 2273;www.universalorlando.com 🕐 Daily ✋ Very expensive

SeaWorld Orlando

✉ 7007 SeaWorld Drive ☎ 407/351-3600 or 1-800 423 3688;

www.seaworld.com ⏰ Daily 9–7 (extended summer and hols) ✋ Very expensive 🍴 Various restaurants ($–$$$) 🚌 I-Ride, Lynx 42

Discovery Cove
✉ 6000 Discovery Cove Way ☎ 407/370-1280 or 1-800 327 2424; www.discoverycove.com ⏰ Daily (check schedules) ✋ Very expensive

Orlando Science Center
✉ 777 E. Princeton Street ☎ 407/514-2000 or 1-800 672 4386; www.osc.org ⏰ Sun–Tue 10–6, Wed–Thu 10–9, Fri–Sat 10–11 ✋ Moderate

Harry P. Leu Gardens
✉ 1920 N. Forest Avenue ☎ 407/246-2620; www.leugardens.org ⏰ Daily 9–5 ✋ Moderate ❓ House tours: daily every 30 mins

PINELLAS SUNCOAST

A 28-mile (45km) strip of hotel-lined barrier island beaches, the Pinellas Suncoast is the busiest resort area on the Gulf coast. The lively districts of St. Pete Beach and Clearwater Beach both make good seaside bases for trips around the Tampa Bay area. From Clearwater Beach boat services go to gorgeous Caladesi Island State Park, a barrier island preserve with one of the finest beaches in the country.

The area has a couple of low-key attractions, the best of which is the **Pinellas County Heritage Village,** a collection of 28 restored historic buildings including pioneer cabins, Edwardian homes, a church and a train station. The Suncoast Seabird Sanctuary rescues pelicans, herons, egrets and other birds.
➕ 13L

Pinellas County Heritage Village
✉ 11909 125th Street N. Largo ☎ 727/582-2123 ⏰ Tue–Sat 10–4, Sun 1–4 ✋ Free (donations welcome)

ST. PETERSBURG
Best places to see, ➤ 48–49.

SARASOTA
Best places to see, ➤ 52–53.

TAMPA
A hopping bayfront city, Tampa offers some of the most varied and exciting attractions on the Gulf coast. Henry Plant brought the railroad to town in 1884 and built a grand hotel to house the expected flood of tourists. The city's prospects improved further with the arrival of Cuban cigar workers in 1886, who established themselves at Ybor City. Plant's lavish Moorish Revival-style hotel

is a local landmark. Its silver onion-domed minarets act as a beacon for visitors crossing the Hillsborough River from downtown to visit the **Henry B. Plant Museum** in a suite of former hotel rooms.

Downtown Tampa is compact and easy to explore on foot. Backing onto the river, the **Tampa Museum of Art** displays fine Greek and Roman antiquities and 20th-century American art, shown in rotation, and hosts traveling exhibitions.

On the waterfront, the terrific **Florida Aquarium** should not be missed. Displays follow a drop of water from the Florida aquifer on its journey to the sea via river and swamp dioramas inhabited by live waterbirds, otters and freshwater fish. There are scurrying crabs in Bays and Beaches, a Coral Reef exhibit with dive demonstrations, and Offshore tanks showcasing local marine life.

Out to the east of the city, Tampa's top crowd-puller is the huge African-inspired **Busch Gardens** theme park, which doubles as one of the nation's premier zoos. More than 3,300 animals roam the central Serengeti Plain and appear in special exhibits such as the Great Ape Domain and the Edge of Africa safari experience. Busch Gardens is also famous for its thrill rides including the inverted roller coaster, Montu; the water-soaking Tanganyika Tidal Wave and Florida's tallest roller coaster SheikRa.

Just down the road from Busch Gardens, the **Museum of Science and Industry** (generally referred to as MOSI) inhabits a striking modern architectural complex. Here, imaginative

interactive displays tackle the mysteries of the world about us and the GTE Challenger Learning Center turns the spotlight on to space travel and research.

www.visittampabay.com

✚ 14L

Henry B. Plant Museum

✉ 401 W. J. F. Kennedy Boulevard ☎ 813/254-1891 ⏰ Tue–Sat 10–4, Sun 12–4 ✋ Donations

Tampa Museum of Art

✉ 600 N. Ashley Drive ☎ 813/274-8130 ⏰ Tue–Sat 10–5 (3rd Thu of month 10–8), Sun 11–5 ✋ Inexpensive

Florida Aquarium

✉ 701 Channelside Drive ☎ 813/273-4000 ⏰ Daily 9:30–5 ✋ Expensive

Busch Gardens

✉ 3000 E. Busch Boulevard (at 40th Street) ☎ 888/800-5447 ⏰ Daily 9:30–6 (extended summer and hols) ✋ Very expensive

Museum of Science and Industry (MOSI)

✉ 4801 E. Fowler Avenue ☎ 813/987-6100 ⏰ Mon–Fri 9–5, Sat and Sun 9–6 ✋ Expensive (IMAX film included in admission)

a walk around Ybor City

Tampa's historic cigar-making quarter has undergone a modest renaissance. Old cigar factories and workers' cottages now house shops, cafés and restaurants, and the weekend club scene is hugely popular. The starting point is Ybor Square, the original red brick cigar factory, which has been transformed into a shopping mall.

Turn left out of the front entrance onto Avenida Republica de Cuba for a short walk to the corner of 9th Avenue.

On the opposite corner are the arcades of the old Cherokee Club, once patronized by Cuban freedom fighter José Martí, Teddy Roosevelt and Winston Churchill.

Turn right for one block on 9th, leading directly to the Ybor City State Museum. It is more fun to walk down 15th Street and along 7th Avenue, or La Septima, Ybor City's main shopping street. Cut back up to 9th Avenue at 18th Street; turn right.

The museum tells the story of the cigar industry and the migrants who came to work here. Down the street, a worker's cottage has been restored.

Cut across the plaza by the Immigrant Statue to 19th Street. Rejoin 7th Avenue, and turn left.

The walk-in humidor at Columbia Restaurant Cigar Store, number 2014, is one of several interesting stops along this section of La Septima. The Columbia Restaurant building, on the corner of 21st Street, is lavishly adorned with hand-painted tiles.

Walk back down 7th Avenue with its fashion stores, design emporiums and gift shops.

Distance 1.5 miles/2.5km
Time 2 hours with stops
Start/end point Ybor Square
Lunch Little Sicily ($) ✉ 1724 8th Avenue E.
(at 18th Street) ☎ 813/248-2940

TARPON SPRINGS

A little piece of Florida that is forever Greek, the sponge fishing center of Tarpon Springs has a distinctly Mediterranean air. Greek divers first came here to harvest the Gulf sponge beds in the early 1900s. In addition to their sponging skills they imported a hefty slice of Greek culture, which today has turned the dockside town into something of a tourist magnet.

Piles of sponges decorate Dodecanese Boulevard, the bustling main thoroughfare, where sidewalk cafés play bouzouki music and sell ouzo. Join one of the narrated boat trips around the docks for a lesson in local history, and drop in on the **Tarpon Springs Aquarium** for a peek at the local marine life. For scrumptious treats, be sure to sample the delicious Greek pastries on sale in a host of bakeries.

www.tarponsprings.com

➕ 13L

Tarpon Springs Aquarium

✉ 850 Dodecanese Boulevard ☎ 727/938-5378 🕘 Mon–Sat 10–5, Sun 12–5 ✋ Inexpensive

VERO BEACH

Chosen by Disney for their first Florida seaside resort, Vero Beach has a reputation for attractive vacation homes, a celebrated arts center and muted luxury. Galleries and boutiques gather on Ocean Drive, near the landmark Driftwood Resort. This eccentric oceanfront property was founded in the 1930s, and is partially constructed from driftwood washed ashore on the beach.

North of town, along the Treasure Coast, the **Sebastian Inlet State Recreation Area** is a favorite with surfers and fishermen. The McLarty Treasure Museum describes how the Treasure Coast got its name when the Spanish Plate Fleet was dashed onto the reefs during a storm in 1715.

✚ 17M

Sebastian Inlet State Recreation Area
✉ 9700 S A1A ☎ 321/984-4852 🕐 24 hours. Museum: 10–4 👋 Inexpensive

© Disney

WALT DISNEY WORLD® RESORT

Walt Disney World® Resort is truly a world within a world. The biggest entertainment complex on the planet is made up of four theme parks, two water parks, and enough shopping, dining and nightlife to keep the family entertained full time. Around 23 million guests visit Walt Disney World® Resort annually, and it can get extremely busy. Avoid vacation periods if you can; the most comfortable times to visit are mid-September until mid-December, and January until mid-February. The Disney experience does not come cheap, but tickets can be purchased ahead, which helps with planning as well as cutting down on lining up at the gates; reservations for accommodations should be made well in advance.

The following is a brief guide to the best of Walt Disney World® Resort.

http://disneyworld.disney.go.com

🚑 15K ✉ Lake Buena Vista (20 miles/32km south of Orlando)
☎ Information: 407/939-4636; reservations: 407/934-7639 ⏰ Check current schedules 👋 Very expensive 🍴 Each park offers a choice throughout the day. Make reservations at Guest Relations for table service restaurants ($$–$$$) 🚌 Free bus from many Orlando/Kissimmee hotels. Walt Disney World® transportation operates from the Magic Kingdom® ticketing center ❓ Details of parades, shows, fireworks and laser displays are in park guides

FASTPASS®

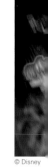
© Disney

Beat the lines with the time-saving Disney FASTPASS® designed to cut waiting times on the most popular rides in all four parks. Insert your admission ticket into the FASTPASS® machines at the rides offering the complimentary service and you'll receive a designated ride time.

Ticket Options

For short-stay visitors, the only ticket option available is one-day one-park tickets. For longer stay visitors, and those planning to return later on in their vacation, 5 and 7 Day Park Hopper Plus Passes offer unbeatable flexibility,

isney

plus savings on single-day tickets. The passes cover unlimited admission to all four theme parks and a choice of entries to the water parks, Pleasure Island and Disney's Wide World of Sports® Complex. Pass-holders are free to hop from park to park on the same day and use the transportation system.

Blizzard Beach and Typhoon Lagoon

Disney's two water parks are enormously popular for a day away from the theme park trail. The biggest and arguably the best is Blizzard Beach with its bizarre ski resort theme and mountainous water slides including the dramatic 60mph (96kph) Summit Plummet slide. Typhoon Lagoon goes for the shipwrecked tropical look, a huge wave-pool lagoon and rafting adventures.

Disney's Animal Kingdom® Park

The largest of the Disney theme parks (five times bigger than the Magic Kingdom®) opened in the spring of 1998. The giant 14-story Tree of Life towers over Discovery Island at the heart of the park, linked by bridges to Africa, Asia, DinoLand U.S.A.® and the small child-friendly Camp Minnie-Mickey. Top rides include Kilimanjaro Safaris into the 100-acre (40ha) African savannah for close

© Disney

encounters with exotic animals and the Expedition Everest; a super-serious, forward-backward, high altitude, steep-pitch roller coaster that'll take you into the Himalayas to encounter the Yeti.

Disney's Hollywood Studios (formerly Disney-MGM Studios)
A fun Hollywood-style setting for rides and shows based on Disney movies. The Backlot Tour and The Magic of Disney animation step behind the scenes of the studio, while live shows draw inspiration from blockbuster successes such as The Voyage of the Little Mermaid and Beauty and the Beast – Live on Stage. The best thrill rides are Twilight Zone™ Tower of Terror and the Rock 'n' Roller Coaster® starring Aerosmith.

Downtown Disney® Marketplace, Pleasure Island and West Side

A mega entertainment district on the shores of Lake Buena Vista, Downtown Disney® encompasses shopping, celebrity restaurants and entertainments. The new Disney West Side attractions include a giant movie theater complex, while the Pleasure Island nightlife zone has no fewer than eight clubs, which run the gamut from 1970s disco hits to country music.

Epcot®

A park in two parts, Disney's Experimental Prototype Community of Tomorrow looks at the world about us. Future World tackles things scientific with typical Disney flair. Highlights include The Living Seas aquarium, the boat ride through experimental gardens in The Land, the fantastic dinosaur romp in Universe of Energy and Spaceship Earth. World Showcase presents 11 pavilions, set around the Lagoon, depicting the potted architecture and culture of nations as diverse as Canada and China.

Magic Kingdom®

Best places to see, ➤ 54–55.

WEEKI WACHEE SPRINGS

One of those truly weird "only in Florida" attractions, this veteran theme park's unique selling point is its underwater ballets performed by live "mermaids." For students of the kitsch it is a must. Less unusual attractions include a wilderness river cruise, a water park with waterslides, riverfront picnic area and beach.

✚ 14K ✉ US19 at SR 50 ☎ 352/596-2062 or 1-800 678-9335 🕙 Daily 9:30–5:30 ✋ Moderate 🍴 Mermaid Gallery (£)

HOTELS

CLEARWATER BEACH
♦♦ Palm Pavilion Inn ($$)
Right on the Gulf, this attractive hotel has various rooms, suites and apartments, with amenities that include TV, air conditioning and safe.

✉ 18 Bay Esplanade ☎ 727/446-6777

KISSIMMEE
♦♦♦ Quality Suites Maingate East ($$)
See page 65.

ORLANDO
♦♦ Best Western Plaza International ($$)
Modern chain hotel with rooms and family suites. Good children's facilities and babysitting service.

✉ 8738 International Drive ☎ 407/345-8195 or 1-800 654 7160

♦♦♦ Hard Rock Hotel ($$$)
See page 65.

ST. PETE BEACH
♦♦♦ Sirata Beach Resort ($$)
Big beachfront property with spacious rooms, a restaurant, lively tiki bar and pool. Water sports rentals are available.

✉ 5300 Gulf Boulevard ☎ 727/363-5100 or 1-800 344 5999

♦♦♦ Trade Winds Sandpiper ($$)
A large hotel in a superb beachfront location. Of the variety of rooms and suites available, the best are those with picture windows and balconies overlooking the Gulf of Mexico.

✉ 6000 Gulf Boulevard ☎ 727/360-5551 or 1-800 237 0707

WALT DISNEY WORLD® RESORT
♦♦ Disney's All-Star Sports, Movie and Music Resorts ($–$$)
See page 65.

❤❤❤ Disney's Caribbean Beach Resort ($$)

Large, comfortable rooms in five tropically landscaped "villages,"
each with a pool and lakeside beach.

✉ 900 Cayman Way ☎ 407/934 3400; reservations, 407/934-7639

RESTAURANTS

CLEARWATER BEACH
❤ Crabby Bill's ($–$$$)

Fresh seafood directly from the Gulf of Mexico is the basis of this
renowned restaurant, the first in a chain of eight in Florida, just
south of Clearwater. Stone crabs (in season) are a huge crowd
puller but for non-fish fanciers there is steak, chicken and ribs.

✉ 401 Gulf Boulevard, Indian Rocks Beach ☎ 727/595-4825 🕐 Lunch
and dinner

COCOA BEACH
❤❤ Black Tulip ($$)

Cozy, fine-dining restaurant in historic Cocoa Village. A
Mediterranean influence can be detected in the pasta dishes
or tuck into steak au poivre. Lunchtime options include soup
and salads.

✉ 207 Brevard Avenue, Cocoa Village ☎ 321/631-1133 🕐 Lunch and dinner

KISSIMMEE
Angels ($–$$$)

Famed locally for its seafood buffet, this restaurant serves just
about every type of American food – head here if your family can't
agree on one particular style of cuisine.

✉ 7300 W. Irlo Bronson Memorial Highway (at the Holiday Inn) ☎ 407/397-
1960 🕐 Breakfast, lunch and dinner

Passage to India ($$)

Excellent Indian cuisine including a range of meats, tandoori,
vegetarian and vegan dishes served as hot as you like. Authentic
Indian carved wood decoration in the dining room.

✉ 7618 E. Irlo Bronson Memorial Highway ☎ 863/424-6969 🕐 Lunch
and dinner

Ponderosa Steakhouse ($)

Family restaurant chain serving a very good value all-you-can-eat buffet laden with steak, chicken, seafood, bread and salads.

✉ 5771 W. Irlo Bronson Memorial Highway/US192 ☎ 407/397-2100
🕐 Breakfast, lunch and dinner

ORLANDO
🔷🔷 Bahama Breeze ($$)

See page 58.

🔷🔷🔷 Delfino Vice ($$$)

Authentic Ligurian Italian cuisine based around seafood dishes served on Versace designed tableware, with views over Orlando's interpretation of Portofino Bay. Italian minstrels complete the Mediterranean atmosphere.

✉ 6501 Universal Boulevard, Portofino Bay Hotel ☎ 407/503-1415 (reservations required) 🕐 Dinner

🔷🔷🔷 The Palm ($$$)

The great Palm steakhouse family owned group has found a home in Orlando. The restaurant serves up perfectly cooked fillets and chops, plus chicken, seafood and salads, in an upscale family oriented environment.

✉ 5800 Universal Boulevard at the Hard Rock Hotel ☎ 407/503-7256
🕐 Dinner

🔷🔷 Race Rock ($$)

Car racing-theme decor, with whole cars, bikes and giant trucks, plus rock music and burgers, pizzas, pasta, Tex-Mex and more.

✉ 8986 International Drive ☎ 407/248-9876 🕐 Lunch and dinner

ST. PETE BEACH
🔷🔷 Sea Critters Café ($–$$)

Casual dockside dining on the waterfront deck or indoors. Tasty menu includes hot fish sandwiches, seafood pasta, Cajun blackened chicken salad and Jamaican jerk.

✉ 2007 Pass-a-Grille Way ☎ 727/360-3706 🕐 Lunch and dinner

💎💎 Leverock's ($$)

One of 10 locations in Florida. Here you can gaze out at the sea while you eat succulent seafood so fresh that was out there swimming around just a short while ago. There are a few meat dishes on the menu too.

✉ 10 Corey Avenue ☎ 727/367-4588 🕐 Lunch and dinner

The Moon Under Water ($$)

See page 58–59.

TAMPA
💎💎💎 Bern's Steak House ($$$)

Juicy prime steaks and organic vegetables are the trademarks at this clubby local legend. Reservations are recommended.

✉ 1208 S. Howard Avenue ☎ 813/251 2421 🕐 Dinner

💎💎 Buca di Beppo ($$–$$$)

See page 58.

💎💎💎 P. F. Chang's China Bistro ($–$$)

Enjoy superlative dishes in a classy, contemporary environment. Lettuce wraps, orange peel chicken and Mongolian beef are among the standards, and their "hot fish" (crispy slices of fish in a Sichuan sauce with stir-fried vegetables) is a standout.

✉ 219 Westshore Plaza ☎ 813/289-8400 🕐 Lunch and dinner

WALT DISNEY WORLD® RESORT
💎💎 Rainforest Café ($$–$$$)

An amusement park attraction in its own right, this jungle-theme restaurant in a mini volcano provides its own microclimate and wildlife, as well as an American menu with a Caribbean twist.

✉ Downtown Disney® (Village Marketplace), 1800 E. Buena Vista Drive ☎ 407/827-8500 🕐 Lunch and dinner

SHOPPING

Downtown Disney® Marketplace
See page 71.

Florida Mall
Central Florida's largest shopping destination with over 250 stores and restaurants and five department stores.
✉ 8001 S Orange Blossom Trail/US441 ☎ 407/851-6255

Historic Cocoa Village
See page 71.

International Plaza
Almost 200 stores and Bay Street outdoor village with a range of restaurants and cafés make this mall a little different from others.
✉ Corner of Boy Scout Boulevard and West Shore Boulevard, Tampa
☎ 813/342-3790

Lake Buena Vista Factory Stores
Over 30 factory outlet stores close to Walt Disney World® Resort. Get 20 to 75 percent discounts on sportswear, jeans and more.
✉ 15591 S. Apopka-Vineland Road/SR535, Orlando ☎ 407/238-9301

Mall at Millenia
See page 71.

Merritt Square Mall
Space Coast mall with more than 80 specialty stores and restaurants and a 16-screen theater.
✉ 777 E. Merritt Island Causeway/SR520, Cocoa Beach ☎ 321/452-3272;
www.merrittsquaremall.com

Old Hyde Park Village
This tree-shaded shopping village is a pleasant place to browse. It boasts some 60 boutiques as well as restaurants and a cinema.
✉ Swann and Dakota Avenues ☎ 813/251-3500

Old Town Kissimmee

There is all the fun of the fair at this Old West style open-air mall, which offers around 70 souvenir stores, clothing and gift shops, plus dining and fairground amusement rides to entertain children.

✉ 5770 W Irlo Bronson Memorial Highway/US192, Kissimmee

☎ 407/396-4888

Park Avenue, Orlando

See page 71.

The Pier

More of a sightseeing feature than a major shopping experience with a variety of small boutiques and stores selling fashion, gifts and souvenirs. There is also dining with waterfront views.

✉ 800 2nd Avenue N.E., St. Petersburg ☎ 727/82-6443; www.stpete-pier.com

Prime Outlets Ellenton

South of Tampa Bay, this is one of the largest factory outlet malls on the coast. More than 135 designer and name-brand stores.

✉ 5461 Factory Shops Boulevard (I-75/Exit 43), Ellenton ☎ 941/723-1150 or 1-888 260 7608

Prime Outlets Orlando

For shopaholics, the vast Belz Factory Shopping World in Orlando exercises all the inexorable pull of a major theme park. There are two full-scale malls and four annexes, containing 170 outlet stores. And that is not all.

✉ 5401 W. Oakridge Road, Orlando ☎ 407/352-9611

St. Armands Circle, Sarasota

See page 71.

ENTERTAINMENT

Arabian Nights

A glittering equestrian dinner show within a Middle Eastern setting.

✉ 6225 W. Irlo Bronson Memorial Highway, Kissimmee ☎ 407/239-9223; www.arabiannights.com

Dolly Parton's Dixie Stampede

Dolly Parton lends her name to this dinner show where the entertainment includes an indoor rodeo with horses, bulls, pigs, ostriches and you can enjoy downhome Southern cooking.

✉ 8251 Vineland Avenue, Orlando ☎ 407/238-4455;
www.dixiestampede.com

Downtown Disney® Pleasure Island

A one-off admission fee covers entry to high-energy, 1970s retro and rock and roll discotheques, comedy and Irish pubs, an adventurers club and punk-rock dance hall.

✉ Downtown Disney®, E. Buena Vista Drive ☎ 407/934-7781
🕐 Nightly until 2am

Green Iguana

A choice of bars, live bands, early evening jazz sessions at the heart of the Ybor City nightlife district.

✉ 1708 E. 7th Avenue, Ybor City, Tampa ☎ 813/248-9555

Metropolis and Matrix

A twin venue with Metropolis providing a sophisticated club atmosphere while the special effects and a multi-million dollar light show at Matrix make this one of the best places to groove.

✉ Pointe Orlando, 9101 International Drive, Orlando ☎ 407/370-3700

Pirate's Dinner Adventure

Partake in a swashbuckling adventure on the high seas at this pirate-themed dinner show.

✉ 6400 Carrier Drive, Orlando ☎ 407/248-0590

Universal CityWalk®

Over 40 restaurants, bars, clubs, a stage for live music, a Hard Rock Café, concert hall and a multiplex cinema make CityWalk an atmospheric place. Pay homage to reggae at Bob Marley – A Tribute to Freedom and enjoy a touch of downtown New Orleans at Pat O'Brien's Orlando. Age restrictions apply at some venues.

✉ Universal Studios®, Universal Boulevard, Orlando ☎ 407/363-8000

Tallahassee

Jacksonville

North Florida

Northern Florida is the cradle of the state, where 16th-century Spanish explorers, pioneer adventurers and plantation owners put down roots long before the advent of the railroad. Bordered by Georgia and Alabama, the north has a distinctly Old South feel, particularly in the Panhandle, where attitudes are more old-fashioned and antebellum architecture nestles beneath giant live oaks.

Between Pensacola and the fishing villages and marshlands of the Big Bend, the Panhandle's blinding quartz sand beaches are the most spectacular in the state. Inland are glassy clear streams and rivers, such as the famous Suwannee.

The other face of the north is the First Coast, which unfurls along the Atlantic shore between the strikingly dissimilar resorts of

cosy Fernandina Beach, historic St. Augustine and bold-as-brass Daytona – all easily reached from Orlando.

Although it's perhaps the least-visited part of the state, Florida's northern Panhandle may be the most pleasing destination. Thick forests, natural springs, unlimited beaches, quiet small towns and comforting back roads are all that's good about the state – a state where these simple pleasures are disappearing rapidly.

APALACHICOLA

Florida's premier oyster producer, this delightful small town lies at the mouth of the Apalachicola River, which feeds the nutrient-rich oyster beds in the bay. Down by the docks, the old brick cotton warehouses stand testament to Apalachicola's days as a thriving 19th-century customs post, and around town there are dozens of gracious old homes built by successful merchants. There is no beach, but St. George Island has a beautiful strip of barrier island shore across the causeway from Eastpoint.

www.apalachicolabay.org

✚ 6E ❓ Walking tour maps available from the Chamber of Commerce, 122 Market Street ☎ 850/653-9415. Florida Seafood Festival, Nov

CEDAR KEY

At the southern extent of the Big Bend, where the Panhandle meets the Florida peninsula, this quirky and weatherbeaten fishing village looks out over the Gulf of Mexico from the tail end of a string of tiny island keys. It is a laid-back retreat for fishermen and birdwatchers with boat trips, seafood restaurants, and a funny little museum telling the story of the 19th-century logging boom that cleared the namesake cedar forests.

This is also a good base for trips to **Manatee Springs State Park,** a favorite wintering spot for manatees, with hiking paths and canoe trails on the Suwannee River.

✚ 13J

Manatee Springs State Park

✉ SR320 (6 miles/9.5km W of Chiefland) ☎ 352/493-6072 ⏰ Daily 8–dusk ✋ Inexpensive

DAYTONA

Daytona's love affair with the combustion engine dates back to the early 1900s, when the likes of Henry Ford, Louis Chevrolet and Harvey Firestone flocked south to enjoy the winter sunshine. Today, the "World Center of Racing" divides its attractions between the hotel-lined sands of Daytona Beach and mainland Daytona across the Halifax River.

Daytona Beach's chief attraction is the broad sandy shore, which is fully geared up for water sports and old-time family fun. There are amusement arcades, fishing, dining and aerial gondola rides on Ocean Pier, cotton candy and go-carts on The Boardwalk, and an open-air bandshell. A rather bizarre selling point is that you can drive along the beach for a small fee, though speeds are nothing like those of the racers that broke the world land speed record here during the pioneer days of car racing.

On the mainland, the biggest crowd-puller is Daytona International Speedway, home of the Daytona 500 and a state-of-the-art visitor center, **DAYTONA USA.** This is speed heaven with a range of interactive exhibits, loads of memorabilia, a behind-the-scenes racing movie and track tours on non-race days.

The **Museum of Arts and Sciences** has something for everyone. Children love the 130,000-year-old giant sloth skeleton and "hands-on" artifacts; there is also a superb collection of fine and decorative American arts and crafts in the Dow Gallery, plus a notable Cuban Museum, spotlighting Latin American culture from 1759 to 1959.

South of Daytona Beach, the **Ponce Inlet Lighthouse Museum** is a popular outing. Built in 1887, the 175ft (53m) tower affords far-reaching views along the coast. Down below, the old keeper's quarters display historical and nautical exhibits, and a special building houses a superb 17ft-tall (5m) first order Fresnel lens, which resembles an enormous glass and brass pine cone.

✚ 16J ❓ Speedweeks/Daytona 500, Feb; Bike Week, Mar; Biketoberfest, Oct

DAYTONA USA
✉ 1801 W. International Speedway Boulevard ☎ 386/947-6800;
www.daytonausa.com ⏰ Daily 9–6 ✋ Expensive

Museum of Arts and Sciences
✉ 352 South Nova Road ☎ 386/255-0285 ⏰ Daily Mon–Sat 9–5, Sun 11–5
✋ Inexpensive

Ponce Inlet Lighthouse Museum
✉ 4931 S. Peninsula Drive ☎ 386/761-1821 ⏰ Daily 10–6 ✋ Inexpensive

DESTIN
Destin revels in the title of the "World's Luckiest Fishing Village."
At the eastern end of the Emerald Coast, where the Gulf waters
are indeed an incredible green, local marinas harbor the largest
fleet of charter fishing boats in Florida, and trophy catches include
blue marlin, tarpon and wahoo. If putting out to sea in boats is not
your thing, there is still the
opportunity to impress –
sizeable tarpon have been
hooked off the 1,200ft (360m)
Okaloosa Pier.

✚ 3C 🛈 Destin Chamber of
Commerce, 4484 Legendary Drive
☎ 850/837-6241;
www.destinchamber.com ❓ Fishing
Rodeo and Seafood Festival, Oct

EDEN GARDENS STATE PARK AND MANSION

This charming antebellum-style mansion was built on the banks of the Choctawhatchee River by logging baron William H. Wesley in 1897. The house has been meticulously restored and furnished with antiques. Outside, shaded by towering southern magnolias and live oaks draped with Spanish moss, picnickers gather on the riverbank. One of the best times to visit is in spring, when the azaleas and camellias are in flower.

www.floridastateparks.org

⊞ 4C ⊠ SR395, Port Washington ☎ 850/231-4214 ⊘ Gardens: daily 8–dusk. House: guided tours Thu–Mon 9–4 ✋ Gardens: free. House: inexpensive (small parking fee)

FERNANDINA BEACH

At the northern corner of Amelia Island, facing Georgia across the Amelia River, Fernandina is a charming small resort and fishing center famous for its 50-block Victorian Historic District.

At the heart of town, Centre Street leads down to the wharves, where the shrimping fleet docks. Quiet streets are lined with a lexicon of Victorian architectural styles from Queen Anne homes and Italianate villas to ornate Chinese Chippendale creations. Many of these are now bed-and-breakfast inns, and there are several luxurious resorts on the island.

Fernandina's checkered past is unraveled in the **Amelia Island Museum of History.** This strategic site has been fought over so many times it is known as the Isle of Eight Flags, and oral history

tours of the museum are illustrated with centuries-old Timucua Indian artifacts and Spanish colonial relics. There is more history in store at **Fort Clinch State Park** where rangers adopt Civil War uniforms and take part in monthly historic re-enactments. In the grounds there are hiking trails, beaches, and a campsite.

🕇 12C

Amelia Island Museum of History

✉ 233 S. 3rd Street ☎ 904/261-7378; www.ameliamuseum.org
🕓 Mon–Sat 10–5, tours at 11 and 12, Sun 1–4 ✋ Inexpensive

Fort Clinch State Park

✉ 2601 Atlantic Avenue ☎ 904/277-7274 🕓 Daily 8–dusk ✋ Inexpensive

FLORIDA CAVERNS STATE PARK

This state park offers a rare opportunity to explore Florida's limestone foundations through a series of stunning underground caverns. Around 65ft (20m) below ground, the caverns are decorated with eerily beautiful stalactites and stalagmites and maintain a cool 61–66°F (16–19°C). Above ground, there are woodland hiking trails and bridle paths, a swimming hole on the Chipola River and a 52-mile (84km) canoe trail, which follows the river south to the Apalachicola National Forest.

✚ 5C 🍴 Limited in Marianna; concession in the park

Florida Caverns State Park

✉ 3345 Caverns Road (off SR167)

☎ 850/482-9598;

www.floridastateparks.org 🕐 Oct–Feb daily 8–dusk; Mar–Sep daily 8–4:30

✋ Inexpensive

FORT WALTON BEACH

The western anchor of the Emerald Coast, which stretches east in a 24-mile (39km) swathe of dazzling quartz sand to Destin (► 157), Fort Walton is a well-developed family resort, very safe swimming, water sports, fishing and golf. As well as the glories of the beach, there is marine life entertainment at the **Gulfarium.** Regular dolphin and sea lion shows are interspersed by aquarium displays, the Living Sea exhibit with its sharks and sea turtles, free-ranging exotic birds and enclosures for alligators and 600-pound (270kg) gray seals.

North of the town, across Choctawhatchee Bay, the enormous Eglin Air Force Base welcomes visitors to the **US Air Force Armament Museum,** the only museum in the US dedicated to Air Force weaponry. Top exhibits include an SR-71 "Blackbird" spy plane. The Theater holds regular film show, *Arming the Air Force*, relating the history of the base which controls a large flight test area above the Gulf of Mexico.

✚ 3C

Gulfarium
✉ 1010 Miracle Strip Parkway/US98 E
☎ 850/243-9046 🕐 Jun–Aug daily 9–6, Sep–May daily 9–4 ✋ Expensive

US Air Force Armament Museum
✉ Route 85, Eglin Air Force Base
☎ 850/882-4062 🕐 Daily 9:30–4:30
✋ Free

GAINESVILLE
A pleasantly leafy university town, Gainesville is home to the University of Florida and its 2007 national champions, the Gators football team. Football weekends are to be avoided unless you are a fan, but otherwise head for the campus, where two of Gainesville's highlights are to be found.

First stop is the excellent **Florida Museum of Natural History,** which covers both the history and geography of the state. It has an excellent gallery devoted to pre-Columbia Calusa Indians and exhibits relating to Indian societies in the present day.

The neighboring **Samuel P. Harn Museum of Art** is another campus crown jewel with impressive collections of ancient and modern arts and crafts from Europe, Asia, Africa and South America as well as the Chandler Collection of American Art. The collections have to be shown in rotation, and they frequently make way for high-profile traveling exhibitions.

Southwest of the town, the Kanapaha Botanical Gardens are a tranquil spot, with a hummingbird garden and woodland paths where spring flowers, azaleas and camellias bloom early in the year. In summer, giant Amazon water lily pads float on the lake like 5ft-wide (1.5m) mattresses, and a tangle of honeysuckle, clematis, passion flowers and jasmine wreathes the arches of the fragrant vinery.

Another interesting side trip is the Devil's Millhopper State Geological Site. The 50ft-wide (150m) sinkhole was caused by the collapse of the thin limestone crust covering an underground cavern. A 232-step staircase winds down into its cool 120ft (36m) fern-flanked recesses, watered by a dozen miniature waterfalls.

✚ 10E

Florida Museum of Natural History

✉ Hull Road (off SW 34th Street) ☎ 352/846-2000 ⏰ Mon–Sat 10–5, Sun and holidays 1–5 ✋ Free

Samuel P. Harn Museum of Art

✉ Hull Road ☎ 352/392-9826 ⏰ Tue–Thu 11–5, Sat 10–5, Sun 1–5 ✋ Free

GRAYTON BEACH

At this rare low-key seaside enclave on the Panhandle shore, are pine-shaded family vacation homes fronted by a magnificent stretch of beach. Preserved by the **Grayton Beach State Recreation Area,** it is often ranked in the top ten beaches in the US.

Just east of town, the whimsical Old Florida-style resort of Seaside is a local landmark and tourist attraction. It was used as the location for the supernaturally perfect community in 1998 film

The Truman Show. Ostentatiously cute Victorian-inspired cottages with gingerbread trim and picket fences line the narrow red-brick paths, which are reserved for the use of spookily silent golf carts.
✚ 4C

Grayton Beach State Recreation Area
✉ CR30–A (off US98) ☎ 850/231-4210 ⏱ Daily 8–dusk ✋ Inexpensive

JACKSONVILLE

Founded on the St. Johns River in 1822, and named for General Andrew Jackson, the first governor of Florida, Jacksonville is the huge and high-rise capital of the First Coast. This was the original tourist gateway to Florida, though today's visitors tend to head for the Jacksonville Beaches, 12 miles (19km) east of downtown, and visit the city's several attractions on day trips.

The heart of the city spans a bend in the river, with the business district and Jacksonville Landing shopping and restaurant complex on the north bank. It is linked to the Riverwalk on the south bank by a water taxi, a convenient route to the **Museum of Science and History.** This is the place to learn about the natural history of the state in Currents of Time, which charts 12,000 years of Jacksonville's story. Other exhibits include The Florida Naturalists Center displaying more than 60 native species of animals and plants, plus The Universe of Science interactive exhibit.

The **Cummer Museum of Art and Gardens** is worth the trip into Jacksonville alone. In the attractive Riverside residential district, it contains the finest art collection in the northeast, ranging from medieval and Renaissance European art to 20th-century American works, and from pre-Columbian antiquities to Meissen porcelain. The English and Italian gardens behind the museum face onto the river, shaded by a superb spreading live oak tree.

To the north of the city, **Jacksonville Zoo** has more than 800 animals and birds including Florida panthers, lions, elephants, apes and giraffes. The Range of the Jagua comes complete with an authentic rain forest environment. A minitrain chugs around the 73-acre (29ha) site and there are animal encounter presentations.

On the banks of the St. Johns River, **Fort Caroline National Memorial** marks the spot where French colonists attempted to establish a toehold in Florida in 1564. Timucua Indians helped the expeditionary force to build a wooden fort, but it was destroyed by the Spanish the following year. Today there is a reproduction of the 16th-century fort, and woodland nature trails.

The Jacksonville Beaches stretch from Atlantic Beach down to the golfing resorts of Ponte Vedra Beach. On the oceanfront at the **Kathryn Abbey Hanna Park** the beach is backed by dunes and a woodland preserve with trails, fishing and a campground.

✚ 11D ❓ Jacksonville Jazz Festival, Apr

Museum of Science and History
✉ 1025 Museum Circle ☎ 904/396-6674 🕓 Mon–Fri 10–5, Sat 10–6, Sun 1–6 ✋ Moderate

Cummer Museum of Art and Gardens
✉ 829 Riverside Avenue ☎ 904/356-6857 🕓 Tue–Fri 10–9, Sat–Mon 10–5 ✋ Inexpensive

Jacksonville Zoo
✉ 8605 Zoo Parkway (off Heckscher)
☎ 904/757-4463 🕓 Mon–Fri 9–5, Sat–Sun 9–6 ✋ Moderate

Fort Caroline National Memorial
✉ 12713 Fort Caroline Road ☎ 904/641-7155 🕓 Daily 9–5 ✋ Free

Kathryn Abbey Hanna Park
✉ 500 Wonderwood Drive ☎ 904/249-4700
🕓 Daily 8–dusk ✋ Inexpensive

a drive the Buccaneer Trail

The Buccaneer Trail follows the A1A coast road from the Jacksonville Beaches north to Fernandina Beach. The start point for this drive is the Mayport Ferry, which makes the short journey across the St. Johns River to Fort George Island every 30 minutes from 6:15am to 10:15pm.

On reaching Fort George Island, turn right on the A1A. After 3 miles (5km) turn left and continue to the Kingsley Plantation.

Dating from 1798, Florida's oldest plantation home was bought by Zephaniah Kingsley in 1814. The plantation grew Sea Island cotton, sugar cane, citrus and corn and was worked by around 60 slaves. A neat row of 23 former slave quarters has survived in a clearing in the woods.

Turn left back onto A1A, and head north to the entrance to Little Talbot State Park.

This quiet preserve offers a choice of marsh and coastal hammock walks and miles of unspoiled beach dunes. Look for otters and marsh rabbits, and the bird life.

Continue northward on A1A, which crosses a causeway over the Nassau Sound to reach Amelia Island.

Amelia Island was named after George II's daughter during a brief period of English rule in 1735. Just 13 miles (21km) long and 2.5 miles (4km) at its broadest point, the island's beaches and the pretty town of Fernandina Beach (▶ 158–159), make it an appealing, relaxed vacation spot.

The quickest route back to the Jacksonville Beaches is to retrace your route down A1A south. Alternatively, take A1A west to join I-95 south for Jacksonville.

Distance 25 miles/40km
Time Allow a full day with stops
Start point Mayport ✚ 12D
End point Fernandina Beach ✚ 12C
Lunch Marché Burette ($) ✉ Amelia Island Resort ☎ 904/261-6161

MICANOPY

The picture-perfect village of Micanopy with its old brick stores and Victorian homes dozes in the shade of magnificent live oaks planted in a canopy over Cholokka Boulevard. The store fronts may have been quietly hijacked by antiques and curio dealers and the grand Herlong Mansion transformed into a comfortable bed-and-breakfast, but this is a lovely corner of Old Florida. It is a good base for a trip to the **Marjorie Kinnan Rawlings State Historic Site,** a fascinating Cracker homestead where the Pulitzer prizewinning writer lived during the 1930s and 1940s.

✚ 14H

Marjorie Kinnan Rawlings State Historic Site

✉ CR325, Cross Creek ☎ 352/466-3672 ⏰ Park: daily 9–5. House tours: Oct–May Thu–Sun 10, 11, 1, 2, 3, 4

✋ Inexpensive

MILTON

Milton is the launch point for a selection of the finest canoeing trails in the state. Several operators offer a range of options from half-day rowing and inner tube rides to three-day expeditions on the Coldwater and Blackwater rivers and Sweetwater and Juniper creeks. Canoe rental can also be arranged from outposts near **Blackwater River State Park.** Here there are hiking trails in the woodlands and swimming in the gently flowing sand-bottomed river, which has sandy beaches along its banks.

✚ 2C 🍴 Café ($)

Blackwater River State Park

✉ 7720 Deaton Bridge Road, Holt. Off US90 (15 miles/24km northeast of Milton) ☎ 850/983-5363 ⏰ Daily 8–dusk

✋ Inexpensive

NATIONAL MUSEUM OF NAVAL AVIATION

Best places to see, ➤ 42–43.

PANAMA CITY BEACH

Chief resort of the "Redneck Riviera," so called for its enormous popularity with vacationers from the neighboring Southern states, Panama City Beach fronts 27 miles (43km) of broad white sands with a wall of hotels, motels and condominiums. Strung out along this "Miracle Strip" are amusement parks and arcades, miniature golf courses, shopping malls and family restaurants. Beachfront concessions offer a host of water sports activities.

Shipwreck Island is a 6-acre (2.4ha) water park with fast slides and water tubes and a slow-moving Lazy River. The unusual Museum of Man in the Sea showcases the development of

underwater breathing and diving equipment (some from the 1600s) as well as treasure from doomed Spanish ships.

Panama City Beach has two animal attractions. **Gulf World** concentrates on marine life, with dolphin and sea lion shows, a walk-through shark tank and assorted aquariums. The small, but well-tended, **ZooWorld** attraction is home to more than 300 animals including bears, big cats, apes and alligators. More than 15 of the animal species here are on the rare and endangered list. There is also a petting zoo.

A welcome escape from the busy main beach, **St. Andrews State Recreation Area** offers unspoiled dunes, woodland trails, fine swimming and diving in the shallows. Regular boat trips go to Shell Island for more lazing around on the beach or gentle shell collecting. Shell Island trips are also available from the Treasure Island and Captain Anderson's marinas.
➕ 4D

Shipwreck Island
✉ 12000 Front Beach Road ☎ 850/234-0368; www.shipwreckisland.com 🕓 Jun–early Sep daily 10:30–5; Mid-Apr to May Sat–Sun 10:30–5 ✋ Expensive

Gulf World
✉ 15412 Front Beach Road ☎ 850/234-5271 🕓 Daily 9–4 ✋ Expensive

ZooWorld
✉ 9008 Front Beach Road ☎ 850/230-1065; www.zoo-world.us 🕓 Daily 9–dusk ✋ Moderate

St. Andrews State Park
✉ 4607 State Park Lane, off Thomas Drive ☎ 850/233-5140; www.floridastateparks.org 🕓 Daily 8–dusk ✋ Inexpensive

PENSACOLA

Spanish explorer Tristan de Luna made the first attempt to establish a colony at Pensacola in 1559, but the capital of the western Panhandle has to content itself with the title of second most historic town in Florida after St. Augustine. However, Pensacola does claim to be the "Cradle of Naval Aviation," and it is home to the excellent National Museum of Naval Aviation (► 42–43).

The British laid out the city center in the 1770s, but most of the buildings in the **Historic Pensacola Village** date from the mid-19th-century timber boom era. A stroll around these tree-shaded streets and squares is a great way to spend half a day or so. There are small museums of local history, industry and commerce, a wealth of Victorian architecture and tours around the interiors of a handful of restored homes.

A few blocks away is the excellent **T. T. Wentworth Jr. Florida State Museum.** A salesman, politician and collector par excellence, Wentworth's hoarding initiated exhibits that cover west Florida's history, archaeology and architecture. There is also a child-pleasing hands-on science museum. A great source of information on Pensacola history, check out the exhibit comparing the affects of 2004's Hurricane Ivan to an equally destructive hurricane that ravaged the town in 1926.

Across Pensacola Bay, the seafront resort of Pensacola Beach was hard-hit by Ivan, but most hotels and restaurants have re-opened and – absent a hurricane – it's a charming place to lay back and enjoy the sun and smooth Gulf waters.

East of Gulf Breeze **The ZOO** houses an exotic menagerie, including white Bengal tigers and snow leopards. The miniature train rides are fun for children and there is a very good animal petting area.

www.visitpensacola.com

✚ 2C ❓ Fiesta of Five Flags, Jun

Historic Pensacola Village

✉ Visitor Center, 205 E. Zaragoza Street ☎ 850/595-5985; www.historicpensacola.org ◷ Mon–Sat 10–4 ✋ Moderate

T. T. Wentworth Jr. Florida State Museum

✉ 1330 S Jefferson Street ☎ 850/595-5990 ◷ Mon–Sat 10–4 ✋ Free

The ZOO

✉ 5701 Gulf Breeze Parkway ☎ 850/932-2229 ◷ Daily 9–5 ✋ Moderate

ST. AUGUSTINE

Best places to see, ➤ 46–47.

TALLAHASSEE

Diplomatically sited midway between the two historic cities of
St. Augustine and Pensacola, the state capital is a fine old
Southern town just 14 miles (23km) from the Georgia border.
Tallahassee radiates from the hilltop Capitol Complex, where the
Old Capitol (built in 1845 but restored to its 1902 appearance)
crouches in the shadow of its towering modern successor. Both
are open to visitors, and the Old Capitol has a number of
interesting historic exhibits.

It is a short stroll to the quiet tree-lined streets of the Park
Avenue historic district where 19th-century legislators and
merchants built gracious homes. Tour maps for self-guided walks
are available from the Capitol Complex visitor center and there are
tours of the charming Knott House Museum in a restored
1840s house.

Another downtown attraction is the **Museum of Florida
History.** Mastodon bones, historical dioramas, and colonial,
pioneer and Civil War artifacts illustrate a colorful and informative

potted history of the state. However,
the museum most likely to appeal to
young children is the terrific
**Tallahassee Museum of History and
Natural Science** out in the woods on
the shores of Lake Bradford. Laid out
in three main areas, the open-air site
contains Big Bend Farm, where
volunteers in pioneer costume work
the 1880s farm with its animals and
crop gardens. Down by the water, a
boardwalk trail leads past enclosures
for Florida wildlife including bobcats
and black bears. A third section
preserves a selection of interesting
historic buildings.

A favorite excursion from Tallahassee is a visit to the **A. B. Maclay State Gardens,** just north of the city. These glorious gardens were founded in the 1930s by Alfred B. Maclay, and surround his winter home. Naturally, the gardens look their best in the cooler months from December (when the first camellias bloom) until April. In the grounds there is boating on Lake Hall, woodland nature trails and picnicking facilities.

➕ 7C ❓ Walk tour maps from the Visitors' Center, New Capitol Building (West Plaza Level)

Old Capitol

✉ S. Monroe Street at Apalachee Parkway ☎ 850/487-1902 🕓 Mon–Fri 9–4:30, Sat 10–4:30, Sun and holidays 12–4:30 ✋ Free

Museum of Florida History

✉ 500 S. Bronough Street ☎ 850/245-6400 🕓 Mon–Fri 9–4:30, Sat 10–4:30, Sun and hols 12–4:30 ✋ Free

Tallahassee Museum of History and Natural Science

✉ 3945 Museum Drive ☎ 850/576-1636; www.tallahasseemuseum.org 🕓 Mon–Sat 9–5, Sun 12:30–5 ✋ Moderate

A. B. Maclay State Park

✉ 3540 Thomasville Road/US319 ☎ 850/487-4556 🕓 Park: daily 8–dusk. Gardens: daily 9–5. House: Jan–Apr 9–5 ✋ Inexpensive

WAKULLA SPRINGS STATE PARK

South of Tallahassee, one of the world's biggest freshwater springs bubbles up from the Florida aquifer into a 4.5-acre (1.8ha) pool at the center of the park. Snorkeling, swimming and glass-bottom boat rides provide a first-hand view of the underwater scenery and the water is so clear it is easy to see the bed of the pool 185ft (56m) below. Boat trips on the Wakulla River offer good

wildlife-spotting opportunities. Look for alligators, deer, turtles, osprey and a wide variety of wading birds.

www.floridastateparks.org

➕ 7D ✉ 550 Wakulla Park Drive/SR267 (off US319) ☎ 850/922-3633 🕐 Daily 8–dusk 💵 Inexpensive, boat tours inexpensive 🍴 Concessions ($) and restaurant ($–$$)

WHITE SPRINGS

This small town on the Suwannee River's claim to fame is the **Stephen Foster Folk Culture Center State Park.** Born in Pennsylvania in 1826, Foster never even saw the Suwannee but he did make it famous with *Old Folks at Home* which he wrote in Southern dialect, in 1851.

In the park, a museum displays dolls'-house dioramas depicting several of Foster's other famous songs such as *Oh! Susanna* and *Jeanie With The Light Brown Hair*, there are daily carillon recitals, craft shops and pontoon boat rides on a pretty forest-lined stretch of the Suwannee.

www.whitesprings.org

➕ 10D ✉ US41 N (3 miles/5km east of I-95) ☎ 386/397-2733

Stephen Foster State Park

🕐 Park: daily 8–dusk. Museum: 9–5 💵 Inexpensive 🍴 Café ($)

HOTELS

APALACHICOLA
✧✧✧ Coombs House Inn ($–$$)
See pages 64–65.

✧✧✧ Gibson Inn ($–$$)
On the National Register of Historic Places, this inn is easily identified by its wraparound porches, fretwork and captain's watch. Rooms have four-poster beds, antique armoires, and pedestal lavatories that have wide basins and porcelain fixtures.
✉ 51 Avenue C ☎ 850/653-2191; www.gibsoninn.com

FERNANDINA BEACH
✧✧✧ ✧✧✧ Amelia Island Plantation ($$$)
A superb resort property set in 1,000 acres (404ha) of woodland, beach dunes and golf courses. Lavishly furnished and attractive hotel rooms, condos and villas, fine dining and matchless facilities.
✉ 3000 First Coast Highway ☎ 904/261-6161 or 1-888 261 6161

✧✧✧ Elizabeth Pointe Lodge ($$–$$$)
A grand, New England-style bed-and-breakfast resort on the ocean, giving you the best of America's Southeast and Northeast in one. Only a few blocks from historic Fort Clinch.
✉ 98 S. Fletcher Avenue ☎ 904/277-4851; elizabethpointelodge.com

PANAMA CITY BEACH
✧✧ Days Inn Beach ($$)
Directly on the Gulf of Mexico, this family-friendly hotel provides a free breakfast, plus a swimming pool with a six-story waterfall, high-speed wireless Internet, suites with microwaves, refrigerators (some include kitchenettes) and cable television.
✉ 12818 Front Beach Road ☎ 850/233-3333

PENSACOLA
✧✧ Microtel Inn ($–$$)
If you're more concerned with your budget than extravagances, consider this chain option where the no-frills rooms are small,

small, small (but include cable and WiFi and a continental breakfast), and can help protect a vacation budget.
✉ 8001 Lavelle Way ☎ 850/941-8902

♦♦ Ramada Inn Bayview ($$)

In a secluded setting by the bay, this hotel is arranged around a central swimming pool within leafy gardens. Each of the 150 rooms has a private balcony or patio. Complimentary airport transportation is available.
✉ 7601 Scenic Highway ☎ 850/477-7155

ST. AUGUSTINE
♦♦ Bayfront Inn ($–$$)

Right on the waterfront, this Spanish-style inn with a pool is also close to the historic district attractions, stores and restaurants
✉ 138 Avenida Menendez ☎ 904/824-1681 or 1-800 558 3455

♦♦♦ Casa Monica ($$)

In the heart of the old city, this landmark 1888 building looks just like a Spanish castle. It combines impeccable service with a truly welcoming atmosphere, and rooms are individually furnished.
✉ 95 Cordova Street ☎ 904/827-1888 or 1-800 648 1888

TALLAHASSEE
♦ Econo Lodge ($–$$)

A seriously middle-of-the-road, modest retreat where you can get rest and get refreshed before exploring one of the most intriguing cities in Florida. Rooms come with two double or one queen- or king-sized bed, as well as free local calls, premium TV channels, and a Continental breakfast. If you won't be staying in your room much, give some thought to this.
✉ 2681 N. Monroe Street ☎ 850/385-6155

Governor's Inn ($$–$$$)

See page 65.

✦✦✦ La Quinta Inn ($)

Attractive inn just 2 miles (3.2km) from downtown. Relax after a day in the city. The Continental breakfast buffet is complimentary.

✉ 2905 Monroe Street ☎ 850/385-7172 or 1-800 432 9755

RESTAURANTS

CEDAR KEY
✦✦ Island Hotel ($$)

This historic inn specializes in seafood straight off the docks; treats include blue crabs and clams. Check out the murals in the bar.

✉ 373 2nd Street ☎ 352/543-5111 ⏱ Tue–Sun dinner

FERNANDINA BEACH
✦✦✦ Beech Street Grill ($$$)

Enjoy innovative New American cooking with local seafood and a good wine list in the attractive modern dining rooms of this charming old property in the historic district.

✉ 801 Beech Street ☎ 904/277-3662 ⏱ Dinner

✦✦ Brett's Waterway Café

Overlooking the Amelia River, this a casually elegant restaurant in the heart of the historic district is known for its steaks as well as (naturally) fresh Florida seafood.

✉ 1 South Front Street ☎ 904/261-2660 ⏱ Lunch and dinner

✦✦✦ Florida House Inn ($)

All-you-can-eat boarding house dinners are served up in Florida's oldest hotel. Trestle tables are loaded with home-cooked food.

✉ 20–22 S. 3rd Street ☎ 904/261-3300 ⏱ Tue–Sat lunch and dinner

JACKSONVILLE
✦ Crispers ($)

See page 58.

✦✦ Dolphin Depot ($$)

This very popular and very good seafood restaurant is noted for its excellent daily specials. The Depot dolphin fish (mahi-mahi) with

matchstick sweet potatoes and home-made chutney is a
house specialty.

✉ 704 N. 1st Street, Jacksonville Beach ☎ 904/270-1424 ⏰ Dinner

PANAMA CITY BEACH
♻♻ Boars Head Restaurant ($$$)

An "Olde English" style restaurant the Boars Head specializes in
roasted and chargrilled meats and fresh seafood.

✉ 17290 Front Beach Road ☎ 850/234-6628;
www.boarsheadrestaurant.com ⏰ Dinner

♻♻ Saltwater Grill ($$$)

Seafood's a specialty, with entrees including blue crab stuffed
flounder, grilled Atlantic salmon and grouper imperial sautéed with
sherry butter and topped with fresh lump crabmeat. Add to this
steaks, chicken, chops and a piano bar.

✉ 11040 Hutchison Boulevard ☎ 850/230-2739; www.saltwatergrillpcb.com
⏰ Dinner

♻♻ Sonny's Real Pit Bar-B-Q ($)

Barbeque platters are stacked with all the foods that make
Southern food legendary: ribs, pork (sliced or pulled), chicken,
hamburgers, sweet potatoes, cole slaw, cornbread, baked beans
corn on the cob, banana pudding. The best part: it's cheap.

✉ 11341 Panama City Beach Parkway ☎ 850/230-4742 ⏰ Lunch and dinner

PENSACOLA
♻ Barnhill's ($–$$)

Join the crowd at an endless buffet of big food at a low price.
Load up on an overwhelming selection of steak, chicken, ham,
fish, vegetables, breads, salads and a mammoth dessert bar.

✉ 10 S. New Warrington Road ☎ 850/456-2760 ⏰ Lunch and dinner

♻♻♻ Jaime's ($$$)

At this lovely historic home, with an art deco interior, a wide-
ranging menu draws on Floribbean and Continental influences.

✉ 424 E. Zaragoza Street ☎ 850/434-2911 ⏰ Dinner. Closed Sun

☙☙ McGuire's Irish Pub ($)

A good atmosphere, a busy bar and home-brewed beers. Ribs, burgers, seafood and other favorites on the menu.

✉ 600 E. Gregory Street ☎ 850/433-6789 ⏰ Lunch and dinner

☙☙ Mesquite Charlie's ($$)

When you've had enough of Gulf Coast fish dishes, mosey over to this popular Western-style saloon for cuts of charbroiled meat as small as a filet to the 32-oz (0.9kg) porterhouse (share it with friends).

✉ 5901 N.W. Street ☎ 850/434-0498 ⏰ Dinner

ST. AUGUSTINE

☙☙ A1A Aleworks ($$)

A very popular spot, this combination microbrewery and restaurant will satisfy you whether you want regular food (with a Jamaican/Caribbean twist) or are on a liquid diet. Usually crowded with young locals, it's also a great place to grab a balcony table and enjoy yourself with a view of the bridge and the bay.

✉ 1 King Street ☎ 904/829-2977

☙☙ Gypsy Cab Company ($$)

This independent restaurant across the Bridge of Lions near the northern end of Anastasia Island, does everything right. You can find it by looking for a line outside the door. It's worth the wait. The Gypsy style is called "Urban Cuisine," and the menu of fish, steak, veal and chicken dishes changes almost daily. It's always good.

✉ 828 Anastasia Boulevard ☎ 904/824-8244; www.gypsycab.com ⏰ Lunch and dinner

☙☙☙ 95 Cordova ($$-$$$)

Dishes at this elegant restaurant at the magnificent Casa Monica hotel, reflect the influences of American, Asian, Mediterranean, Caribbean and Moroccan cuisine. The six-course "tasting menu" includes shrimp cocktail, fresh mozzarella, lobster broth, jumbo sea scallops, filet mignon and tiramisu.

✉ 95 Cordova Street ☎ 904/810-6810 ⏰ Lunch and dinner

▼▼▼ Raintree ($$$)

Set in a restored historic building, the Raintree offers friendly service and a well-balanced menu with plenty of fresh seafood and great desserts.

✉ 102 San Marco Avenue ☎ 904/824-7211 ⏱ Dinner

TALLAHASSEE

▼▼▼ Chez Pierre ($$$)

Enjoy special occasion dining in a fine old building, where several dining areas with bold color schemes create a chic environment. The French cuisine is very special too

✉ 1215 Thomasville Road ☎ 850/222-0936 ⏱ Lunch Mon–Sat, dinner daily, except Sun in summer. Sun brunch

▼▼ Columbia Restaurant ($$–$$$)

High ceilings, painted tiles and palm trees evoke an atmosphere perfect for Cuban and South American favorites such as tender baby lamb back ribs glazed with guava sauce; and empanadas filled with spiced ground beef served with roasted corn and black-bean salsa.

✉ 98 St. George Street ☎ 904/824-3341 ⏱ Lunch and dinner

SHOPPING

Beach Street

The restored historic storefronts along downtown Beach Street harbor a collection of specialty shops from antique collectibles to the Angell & Phelps Chocolate Factory (tours and free samples).

✉ Daytona

Cordova Mall

Pensacola's premier shopping center combines more than 140 fashion outlets, specialty shops and restaurants with a selection of department stores including Gayfers and Montgomery Ward.

✉ 5100 N. 9th Avenue at Bayou Boulevard, Pensacola ☎ 850/477-5355

Daytona Flea and Farmer's Market

This sprawling 40-acre (16ha) spread of booths and stands, selling anything and everything from clothing to bric-à-brac at bargain prices, is a popular weekend (Fri–Sun) excursion.

✉ 2987 Bellevue Avenue, Daytona ☎ 386/253-3330

Governor's Square

This popular shopping center provides a wide selection of fashion, sportswear, books, music and gifts, restaurants and four department stores conveniently close to downtown.

✉ 1500 Apalachee Parkway, Tallahassee ☎ 850/877-8106; www.governorssquare.com

Jacksonville Landing

A downtown landmark on the north bank of the St. Johns River, the Landing combines around 65 boutiques, gift shops and specialty stores with a food court and several restaurants.

✉ 2 Independent Drive, Jacksonville ☎ 904/353-1188; www.jackonvillelanding.com

Panama City Mall

This shopping, dining and entertainment complex has more than 90 stores anchored by three department stores, plus a food court, movie theater and family games room.

✉ 2150 Martin Luther King Jr. Boulevard, Panama City Beach ☎ 850/785-9587; www.panama-citymall.com

St. Augustine Outlet Center

Take advantage of discounts ranging from 25 to 75 percent from any of the 90-plus outlet stores at this large mall.

✉ I-95/Exit 95 at SR16, St. Augustine ☎ 904/825-1555; www.premiumoutlets.com

ENTERTAINMENT

Club La Vela

La Vela claims to be the largest nightclub in America. Choose from 15 clubs, a pool and beach area – be prepared for wild nights during Spring Break.

✉ 8813 Thomas Drive, Panama City Beach ☎ www.clublavela.com

Razzle's

Dramatic light shows at this popular club accompany the chart and progressive sounds on the dancefloor.

✉ 611 Seabreeze Boulevard, Daytona Beach ☎ 904/257-6236 ⏰ Daily 8pm–3am

Sluggo's

Three floors of bars, books, games, pool tables and live music at this distinctly wacky but hugely entertaining downtown venue.

✉ 130 Palafox Street, Pensacola ☎ 850/435-0543 ⏰ Tue–Sun 3–3

SPORT

Adventures Unlimited Outdoor Center

Kayak, canoeing, and camping trips in one of the least disturbed areas of Florida. Swift streams pass secluded, sugar-white beaches through the Blackwater River State Forest.

✉ Tomahawk Landing, SR87 (12 miles/19km N. of Milton) ☎ 850/626-1669

Daytona International Speedway

The 2.5-mile oval is the most popular racetrack in America, and hosts the legendary Daytona 500 in February, the Pepsi 400 in July, and assorted races and events throughout the year. Tours of the track and interactive Daytona USA museum are well worth it.

✉ 1801 W. International Speedway Boulevard ☎ 904/253 RACE

Jacksonville Jaguars

This NFL expansion team took the field in 1995 and have proven themselves to be fan favorites and frequent playoff contenders.

✉ 1 Alltel Stadium Place ☎ 904/633-6050

Blackwater River State Park, Blackwater Canoe Rental

One of the purest sand-bottom rivers in the nation is the highlight of the park, with swimming, fishing, camping, paddling, and walking trails through pristine woods adding to the appeal.

✉ 7720 Deaton Bridge Road, Milton ☎ 850/983-5363

Index

Acknowledgements

The Automobile Association would like to thank the following photographers, companies and picture libraries for their assistance in the preparation of this book.

Abbreviations for the picture credits are as follows – (t) top; (b) bottom; (c) centre; (l) left; (r) right; (AA) AA World Travel Library.

4l Avalon hotel, AA/P Davison; **4c** Taxis, AA/P Bennett; **4r** Palm Beach, AA/P Bennett; **5l** Church St Station, AA/T Souter; **5r** Ocean Drive, AA/J Lyons; **6/7** Avalon Hotel, AA/J Davison; **8/9** Shells, AA/T Souter; **10c** Tropical shrub, AA/J Tims; **10bl** Killer whale, AA/J Davison; **10br** Aeroplane, AA/J Davison; **10/11** Bayside Marketplace, AA/P Bennett; **11t** Palm Beach, AA/L Provo; **11c** Alligator, AA/J Davison; **11b** The home of Ernest Hemingway, AA/L Provo; **12t** Waitress, AA/P Bennett; **12b** Keylime pie, AA/J Tims; **12/3** Seafood restaurant, AA/P Bennett; **13t** Drink vendor, AA/P Bennett; **13b** Produce for sale, AA/J Davison; **14t** Hamburger, AA/J Tims; **14c** Fish and chips restaurant, AA/J Tims; **14b** Waitress, AA/T Souter; **15l** Beer sign, AA/T Souter; **15r** Oranges, Orlando Convention Visitors' Bureau; **15b** American breakfast, AA/P Bennett; **16t** Sunbathing, AA/L Provo; **16b** Heron, AA/J Tims; **17** Hulk rollercoaster, AA/P Bennett; **18** Sunset, AA/P Bennett; **18/9** Manatees, AA/J Davison; **19** Kennedy Space Center, AA/P Bennett; **20/1** Yellow taxis, AA/P Bennett; **25** Wishes Fireworks Show, ©Disney; **27** Lynx bus, AA/P Bennett; **29** Store advertising boards, AA/P Bennett; **31** Policeman, AA/P Bennett; **34/5** Palm Beach, AA/P Bennett; **36/7** Ocean Drive, AA/J Davison; **37** Ocean Drive, AA/L Provo; **38** Kennedy Space Center, AA/T Souter; **38/9** Kennedy Space Center, AA/P Bennett; **39** Kennedy Space Center, AA/P Bennett; **40** Lighthouse in Key West, AA/J Tims; **40/1** Yacht in Key West, AA/J Tims; **41** Indicator on Key West, AA/P Bennett; **42** National Museum of Aviation, AA/J Tims; **42/3** National Museum of Aviation, AA/J Davison; **43** National Museum of Aviation, AA/J Davison; **44** Whitehall Mansion in Palm Beach, AA/L Provo; **45t** Palm Beach, AA/P Bennett; **45b** Worth Avenue, AA/J Tims; **46** Shop in St. Augustine, AA/J Tims; **46/7** Watermill in St. Augustine, AA/N Murphy; **47** St. Augustine, AA/N Murphy; **48/9** St Petersburg Pier, AA/P Bennett; **49** Egret, AA/P Bennett; **50** Captiva Island, AA/ J Tims; **50/1t** Sanibel Island, AA/P Bennett; **50/1b** Captiva Island, AA/J Tims; **52/3t** Dolphin sculpture in Sarasota, AA/J Tims; **52/3b** Ringling Museum of Art, AA/J Tims; **54/5** Main Street, U.S.A. with Cinderella Castle in background, ©Disney; **55** *Liberty Belle* Riverboat on Rivers of America, ©Disney; **56/7** Church Street Station, AA/T Souter; **58/9** Restaurant, AA/T Souter; **60/1** Lifeguard station, AA/J Davison; **61** Beach scene, AA/L Provo; **63** Wet 'n Wild, AA/P Bennett; **64/5** The Breakers, AA/J Tims; **66/7** Fishing, AA/J Tims; **68** Wooden school house in St. Augustine, AA/P Bennett; **69** Oldest Store Museum, AA/P Bennett; **70/1** Mall, AA/T Souter; **72/3** Miami beach, Art deco district, AA/D Lyons; **75** Hooters restaurant in Downtown Miami, AA/P Bennett; **76** Bayside marketplace, AA/P Bennett; **76/7** Coconut Grove, AA/P Bennett; **78** Holocaust Memorial, AA/P Bennett; **79** Lincoln Road, AA/P Bennett; **80** Biltmore Hotel, AA/J Davison; **80/1** Miami Skyline, AA/P Bennett; **81** Fairchild Tropical Garden, AA/L Provo; **82** Miami Metrozoo, AA/J Davison; **82/3** Ocean Drive, AA/D Lyons; **83** Miami Seaquarium, AA/J Davison; **84/5** Parrot Jungle Island, AA/J Davison; **85** Parrot Jungle Island, AA/P Bennett; **86t** Vizcaya Museum and Gardens, AA/J Davison; **86b** Vizcaya Museum and Gardens, AA/J Davison; **95** Fort Lauderdale, AA/J Tims; **96t** Biscayne National Park, AA/J Tims; **96b** Boca Raton, AA/J Tims; **96/7** Mizner Park, AA/J Tims; **98** Corkscrew Swamp Sanctuary, AA/J Tims; **98/9** Birds in the Everglades National Park, AA/J Davison; **99t** Alligator, AA/J Tims; **99b** Everglades National Park, AA/L Provo; **100** Bonsai trees in Morikami Museum and Japanese Garden, AA/P Bennett; **100/1** Palm Beach, AA/L Provo; **102** Fort Lauderdale, AA/P Bennett; **102/3** Fort Lauderdale, AA/L Provo; **103** Stranahan House, AA/J Tims; **104t** Fort Lauderdale, AA/P Bennett; **104b** Stranahan House, AA/J Tims; **105** Henry Ford's Winter Home, AA/P Bennett; **106** Thomas Edison's home, AA/P Bennett; **107** Seal at Islamorada's Theater of the Sea, AA/J Tims; **108** Key Largo, AA/L Provo; **108/9** Bahia Honda State Park, AA/L Provo; **109** Key Deer, AA/L Provo; **110/1t** Marathon, AA/L Provo; **111t** Third Street South, AA/J Tims; **111b** Naples, AA/P Bennett; **112** West Palm Beach, AA/L Provo; **112/3** West Palm Beach, AA/P Bennett; **121** Juno Beach, AA/J Tims; **122/3** Cypress Gardens, AA/T Souter; **124** Fort Pierce, AA/P Bennett; **124/5** Homosassa Springs Wildlife Park, AA/P Bennett; **125t** Alligators, AA/P Bennett; **126** Juno Beach, AA/J Tims; **126/7** Jupiter Island, AA/J Tims; **127** Kissimmee, AA/P Bennett; **128t** Mount Dora, AA/P Bennett; **128b** Ocala, AA/P Bennett; **128/9** Ocala, AA/P Bennett; **130** Jurassic Park River Adventure(r) at Universal's Islands of Adventure®(r). Jurassic Park River Adventure (r) Universal Studios®/Amblin; **130/1** Downtown Orlando, AA/P Bennett; **131** SeaWorld, AA/P Bennett; **132** Orlando Science Center, AA/P Bennett; **133** Pinellas County Heritage Village, AA/J Tims; **134/5** Busch Gardens, AA/P Bennett; **136** Downtown Tampa, AA/J Tims; **136** Tampa, AA/P Bennett; **137** Tampa, AA/P Bennett; **138/9** Old cigar factory, AA/P Bennett; **140** Tarpon Springs, AA/J Tims; **141** Vero Beach, AA/J Tims; **142** Tree of Life® Attraction, ©Disney; **142/3** Rock 'n Roller Coaster® starring Aerosmith, ©Disney; **143** La Nouba™ Show at Cirque du Soleil®, La Nouba by Cirque du Soleil ®; **144** Spaceship Earth, Day, ©Disney; **145** Weeki Wachee Springs Waterpark, AA/P Bennett; **153** Pensacola, AA/P Bennett; **154/5** Apalachicola, AA/P Bennett; **155** Apalachicola, AA/P Bennett; **156/7** Daytona International Speedway, International Speedway Corporation; **157t** Daytona International Speedway, International Speedway Corporation; **157b** Destin, AA/P Bennett; **158** Eden State Gardens and Mansion, AA/P Bennett; **158/9** Fernandina Beach, AA/P Bennett; **159** Fernandina Beach, AA/P Bennett; **160/1** U.S. Air Force Armament Museum, AA/J Davison; **162/3** Seaside, AA/J Davison; **164/5** Jacksonville, AA/P Bennett; **165** Cummer Museum of Art, AA/P Bennett; **166/7** Amelia Island, AA/P Bennett; **168/9** Blackwater River State Park, AA/P Bennett; **170/1** Panama City Beach, AA/J Davison; **171** Panama City Beach, AA/J Davison; **172** Pensacola, AA/P Bennett; **172/3** Pensacola, AA/P Bennett; **174** Tallahassee, AA/P Bennett; **174/5** Museum in Tallahassee, AA/J Tims; **175** Tallahassee, AA/P Bennett; **176/7** Wakulla Springs State Park, AA/J Davison.

Every effort has been made to trace the copyright holders, and we apologise in advance for any accidental errors. We would be happy to apply the corrections in the following edition of this publication.

Sight locator index

This index relates to the maps on the covers. We have given map references to the main sights of interest in the book. Grid references in italics indicate sights featured on town plans. Some sights within towns may not be plotted on the maps.

Dear Reader

Your comments, opinions and recommendations are very important to us. Please help us to improve our travel guides by taking a few minutes to complete this simple questionnaire.

You do not need a stamp (unless posted outside the UK). If you do not want to cut this page from your guide, then photocopy it or write your answers on a plain sheet of paper.

Send to: **The Editor, AA World Travel Guides, FREEPOST SCE 4598, Basingstoke RG21 4GY.**

Your recommendations...

We always encourage readers' recommendations for restaurants, nightlife or shopping – if your recommendation is used in the next edition of the guide, we will send you a **FREE AA Guide** of your choice from this series. Please state below the establishment name, location and your reasons for recommending it.

_____
_____
_____
_____
_____
_____

Please send me **AA Guide** _____

About this guide...

Which title did you buy?

AA _____

Where did you buy it? _____

When? m m / y y

Why did you choose this guide? _____

_____
_____
_____
_____

Did this guide meet your expectations?

Exceeded ☐   Met all ☐   Met most ☐   Fell below ☐

Were there any aspects of this guide that you particularly liked? _____

_____
_____
_____

continued on next page...

Is there anything we could have done better? _____

_____

_____

_____

About you...

Name (*Mr/Mrs/Ms*) _____

Address _____

_____

_____ Postcode _____

Daytime tel nos _____

Email _____

Please only give us your mobile phone number or email if you wish to hear from us about other products and services from the AA and partners by text or mms, or email.

Which age group are you in?
Under 25 ☐   25–34 ☐   35–44 ☐   45–54 ☐   55–64 ☐   65+ ☐

How many trips do you make a year?
Less than one ☐   One ☐   Two ☐   Three or more ☐

Are you an AA member? Yes ☐   No ☐

About your trip...

When did you book? m m / y y   When did you travel? m m / y y

How long did you stay? _____

Was it for business or leisure? _____

Did you buy any other travel guides for your trip? _____

If yes, which ones? _____

_____

_____

Thank you for taking the time to complete this questionnaire. Please send it to us as soon as possible, and remember, you do not need a stamp (*unless posted outside the UK*).

┌───┐
│ **AA** Travel Insurance call 0800 072 4168 or visit www.theAA.com   │
└───┘